The Middle School Writing Toolkit

The Middle School Writing Toolkit

Differentiated Instruction across the Content Areas

Tim Clifford

The Middle School Writing Toolkit: Differentiated Instruction across the Content Areas
By Tim Clifford

Cover and book design: Marble Sharp Studios
Editor: Emily Gorovsky
Cover photo: Getty Images

Library of Congress Cataloging-in-Publication Data
Clifford, Tim, 1959-
The middle school writing toolkit : differentiated instruction across the
content areas / Tim Clifford.
    p. cm.
Includes bibliographical references and index.
ISBN-13: 978-0-929895-75-8 (pbk.)
ISBN-10: 0-929895-75-4 (pbk.)
1. English language--Composition and exercises--Study and teaching (Middle
school) 2. Language arts (Middle school) 3. Individualized instruction.
I. Title.
LB1631.C55 2006
808'.0420712--dc22

                                    2006028765

Maupin House publishes professional resources for K-12 educators. Contact us for tailored, in-school training or to schedule an author for a workshop or conference. Visit www.maupinhouse.com for free lesson plan downloads.

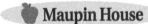 **Maupin House**

Maupin House Publishing, Inc.
2416 NW 71st Place
Gainesville, FL 32653
1-800-524-0634
www.maupinhouse.com

Dedication

This book is dedicated to my wonderful wife, Danna, and my beautiful girls, Katey and Megan. They always knew when to give me time to write and when I needed a hug and a break.

Acknowledgments

I'd like to acknowledge the many people who helped me become a better teacher over the past eighteen years. I learned by watching many wonderful teachers work their magic, each with a different style and dramatic results. I probably borrowed a little from each of them in developing my own style, and I'd like to take this opportunity to thank them.

I've taught a few thousand students over my tenure as an English teacher, and I've learned more about teaching from them than I could ever have imagined.

Thanks also to Janine McGeown, who helped me better understand the challenges and solutions for how-to writing.

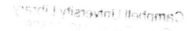

Table of Contents

CHAPTER 7: WRITING A NARRATIVE

CHAPTER 8: WRITING A LITERARY RESPONSE

CHAPTER 9: ORGANIZATIONAL TECHNIQUES: TARGET SKILL LESSONS AND WORKSTATION TASKS

CHAPTER 10: COMPOSING TECHNIQUES: TARGET SKILL LESSONS AND WORKSTATION TASKS

Introduction

Every teacher is a writing teacher.

Until fairly recently, the English teacher was seen as the main, if not the only, teacher of writing. Subject-area teachers tended to focus more on content than the written word. Now that's all begun to change and for the better. Teaching students to write in the content areas just makes sense. Whether you are a subject-area teacher who is new to teaching writing or an English teacher looking for ways to breathe new life into your writer's workshop, this book is for you.

Designed specifically for middle-school teachers, this toolkit offers everything you will need to get your writer's workshop up and running. In all, this book contains fifty-seven writing mini-lessons and more than 200 differentiated workstation tasks that can be easily duplicated and passed out to your students or turned into overheads. You will also find time-saving forms, charts, tasks, and rubrics that should start you well on your way to creating a successful writing program in your classroom.

This book addresses the five major writing genres that middle-school students are expected to master: reports, persuasive essays, how-to (procedural) essays, narratives, and literary responses. There are sections for each of these strands in this book; each section will point you to mini-lessons and tasks that will help your students master the skills necessary to write exemplary papers.

Each section provides you with the essential lessons you need to teach in order to thoroughly explore each strand. These lessons are paired with differentiated workstation tasks that will strengthen the skills of your students at all levels of writing ability.

Also included for each writing strand are sections on the elements of the genre, the challenges of teaching the genre, additional lessons that will spice up student writing, and numerous ways to use each strand across the curriculum. You will also find a task and a rubric for each genre. You can distribute the tasks to your students before drafting begins to let them know your expectations, and you can attach the scoring rubric to each finished writing piece to let students know what areas they need to work on.

If you are new to teaching writing, this book will show you how to become the writing teacher you need to be. More experienced teachers should find plenty of useful material as well, including ways to bring differentiation into your writer's workshop. Let's get started!

HOW TO USE THIS BOOK

Chapter 1. This chapter discusses the challenges facing middle-school writers and how teachers can specifically address the challenge of heterogeneous grouping through differentiated instruction.

Chapter 2. Differentiated instruction is explained further in this chapter, which details the WHAM (Watch, Help, Apply, Master) mini-lesson format and provides advice on assigning differentiated workstation tasks.

Chapter 3. All the information you need to set up your Writer's Workshop is detailed in this chapter.

Chapters 4 through **8.** Each of these chapters discusses one of the five major writing strands or genres: reports, persuasive essays, how-to (procedural) essays, narratives, and literary responses. If you are interested in teaching a specific genre, refer to the chapter for that genre. There, you will find comprehensive instruction on teaching the genre, including which mini-lessons from **Chapters 9** and **10** you will need to teach and a sample writing task and rubric to start you on your way.

Chapters 9 and **10.** The bulk of this book is divided into mini-lessons and workstations for those lessons. The mini-lessons are designed to teach specific Target Skills™ in a time frame of approximately ten minutes. The concept of Target Skills™ Instruction was developed by Marcia S. Freeman in her books, *Building a Writing Community: A Practical Guide* (Maupin House, 1995) and *Listen to This: Developing an Ear for Expository* (Maupin House, 1997), and refers to the set of explicit craft skills that all writers use and that teachers explicitly teach to developing writers one at a time.

After you have taught your mini-lesson to the whole group, your students will go on to their assigned workstation tasks. A workstation is simply a smaller set of students grouped together and practicing the same skill. Often, your groups will be working on the craft lesson you just taught, but some groups may master that skill and be assigned a different workstation instead. For more information on setting up your writer's workshop, including a sample lesson walk-through, see **Chapter 3.**

Workstations are where differentiated instruction takes place. Each mini-lesson is accompanied by four differentiated workstation tasks. Students at the most basic level of the skill are given Task A, the easiest task of the four. You may assign the remaining tasks based upon your assessment of student performance. For a more complete discussion of how to achieve differentiation in your writer's workshop, see **Chapter 2.**

Some of the workstation tasks are differentiated by genre rather than level of difficulty. In these workstations, Task A will be the task specific to reports, Task B will be specific to persuasive essays, and so forth. This was generally done where the need to teach the Target Skill differently for each genre seemed crucial.

Teaching Resources. For ease of use, I have included an index of lessons and workstations for each genre, so there is no need to hunt for what you want. Refer to this section for a list of essential, optional, and advanced craft lessons for each genre. Essential lessons are those that should be taught for each genre, especially when you teach the genre for the first time. Optional lessons give you ideas on how to build craft skills into student writing. Advanced craft lessons may be given to students who have already mastered the skills you are teaching the rest of the class, further differentiating instruction and adding to the writing repertoire of your best writers.

Don't be limited to the genres you are "supposed" to teach. Who says that social studies teachers should teach only persuasive essays and science teachers should teach only procedural essays? Breaking out of that mold often results in some of the most engaging and thoughtful student writing you are likely to see. When social studies teachers have students write personal narratives in the voice of a famous explorer or science teachers have students explain why Thomas Edison would be a good fictional character, real learning takes place. See the "Writing across the Curriculum" section of each genre chapter (**Chapters 4** through **9**) for ideas on making writing come alive in each subject area.

A workstation progress checklist and class evaluation sheet are also included in the **Teaching Resources** section.

A REWARDING CHALLENGE

Teaching writing to middle-school children can be both rewarding and challenging. If you are new to middle school or middle-school writing, make sure to read **Chapter 1**. Despite the challenges, adolescence is an exciting time of growth in the development of young writers. By teaching Target Skills as needed in a differentiated learning environment, you'll witness amazing maturation in student writing.

1

The Challenges Facing Middle-School Writers

If you're reading this book, chances hover near one hundred percent that you emerged from adolescence some time ago and hardly need to be reminded of the tribulations facing middle-schoolers. Yet, as teachers of writing, we need to be mindful of the trials young writers face and plan appropriately. There are three particular problems facing writers making the transition to middle school that this book will address:

- **Adjusting to different instructors and styles of instruction.** In elementary school, students were used to the comfort of a single teacher whose style remained consistent. In middle school, students may have as many as eight or more teachers, each with his or her own curriculum and teaching style. To make matters more confusing, each teacher places a different degree of emphasis on writing. Some may not teach it at all, assuming it to be the realm of the language arts teacher. Some may teach writing skills differently than the child's other teachers. Few schools have a unified approach to teaching writing across the curriculum. This book attempts to help schools find that approach, with chapters addressing each of the five writing strands and lessons that can be used to teach writing in any of the subject areas.

- **Heterogeneous grouping.** Even more so than elementary schools, middle-school classes tend to be comprised of many different types of learners with widely ranging degrees of writing competency. It is virtually impossible to teach a single lesson to a heterogeneous group successfully without tailoring the tasks to the needs of students of differing abilities. This book combines explicit writing instruction through Target Skills with differentiated tasks to allow each student to experience success, whatever his or her level.

- **The need to belong.** Every adolescent has the need to fit into a peer group, particularly in the school environment. Creating an atmosphere in which every student can succeed and celebrate success is critical to teaching middle-school writing. By assigning tasks based upon ability rather than a one-size-fits-all approach, each student should be able to master those tasks. Such victories will lead to a willingness to take risks in the future. The lessons in this book permit students to proceed at their own level of competence and to experience the feeling of achievement that is needed for future growth and experimentation as writers.

Let's take a look how this book addresses each of these problems.

In many middle schools, there is one teacher—the language arts instructor—who is considered to be the writing teacher, while other teachers focus on subject-area content. Yet all teachers evaluate students to a greater or lesser degree on the quality of written work produced. It seems intuitive that all teachers should therefore be teachers of writing.

Research has shown that higher performing schools consciously make connections between the skills being taught and how those skills can be used in the various subject areas (Langer, 2002). Because writing is integral to most subject areas, teaching writing skills across the curriculum seems a great place to start.

A unified approach to writing like the one found in this book can be a key to success. Most of the mini-lessons and tasks found here are not just English lessons; they can be applied across the various writing strands and subject areas. **Chapters 4** through **8** focus on the five major writing strands, including reports, how-to essays, persuasive essays, narratives, and literary responses. Each chapter discusses how to teach the strand across the curriculum. With appropriate planning, a social studies teacher can teach lead types for a persuasive essay, while a science teacher can demonstrate how to write leads for a report. Making connections between skills in the subject areas not only reinforces the skill, it emphasizes the importance of good writing technique in general and improves student performance.

The mini-lessons in this book follow a format called WHAM: Watch, Help, Apply, and Master. The lessons lead students into workstations aimed at their ability level (see **Chapter 2** for a more detailed discussion of WHAM and how it applies to workstations). Using the same lesson format in different subject areas can help facilitate understanding and focus students on writing.

ADDRESSING HETEROGENEOUS GROUPING THROUGH DIFFERENTIATED INSTRUCTION

Truth be told, every class is heterogeneously grouped to some extent. No class can be comprised entirely of students of equal ability with exactly the same skill sets. Therefore, even homogeneously grouped children need lessons and assignments geared towards their own abilities. That need is far more pronounced in heterogeneously grouped classrooms.

Because they are often larger than elementary schools and draw their populations from several schools, middle schools tend to have even more diverse grouping. Gifted students are grouped with those with special needs and everyone in between. This presents difficulties for middle-school teachers and students alike.

In teaching a lesson on similes to a heterogeneously grouped class, for example, there may be some students who can independently incorporate similes into poems and others who don't even know what a simile is. This presents a challenge to teachers because we must instruct all the students in our classes. Do we teach the lesson for the more skilled students and lose the rest, or do we teach it for those new to the skill, and waste the time of the more skilled by revisiting old territory?

For writing instruction to be its most effective, we must do what we can to keep all students engaged in the writing process at all times. The most effective way to do this is through differentiated instruction.

Simply put, differentiation refers to some modification in instruction that allows students to acquire skills at their own pace. These modifications can be to content, process, products, and learning environments (Tomlinson, 2000). This book focuses primarily on content, which Carol Ann Tomlinson defines as "what the student needs to learn or how the student will get access to the information," and process, which includes "activities in which the student engages in order to make sense of or master the content." Toward that end, each mini-lesson in this book is accompanied by four tasks. While some tasks are arranged by genre, the majority are ordered by difficulty, with the first task geared toward learners new to the writing skill and the final task geared toward those able to independently apply the skill. Mini-lessons can be taught to whole groups when necessary or to smaller groups with similar needs.

Chapter 2 contains greater detail on how to achieve differentiation through the use of the mini-lessons and tasks found in this book.

ENCOURAGING ACHIEVEMENT AND RISK-TAKING

Writing is fraught with potential for embarrassment for young writers. As they try out new techniques and methods, they need an environment that fosters achievement and builds confidence. Sharing successful writing pieces is a great way to encourage writers.

Young writers are frequently reluctant to share their writing even with their teachers, let alone to risk embarrassment with their peers. Perhaps the best way to inspire them is to ensure that they are given achievable tasks. Harkening back to the lesson on similes mentioned earlier, students unfamiliar with the technique may be asked only to write a few similes of their own, while more advanced students may be asked to incorporate similes into a poem. Because both students can achieve the goal set for them in the writing task, both can participate in sharing their work at the close of the lesson.

The lessons and tasks in this book, because they scaffold target-writing skills, set students up for success.

In Conclusion

The challenges facing middle-school writers and teachers are daunting at times but not insurmountable. By teaching explicit writing skills, assigning challenging but achievable tasks, and celebrating successes where you find them, you can equip your students with the tools they need to become competent—and even original—writers.

Achieving Differentiation through Workstation Tasks

In an ideal world, educationally speaking, every class would be comprised of students of roughly equal ability and boundless enthusiasm, so that any well-constructed lesson would be absorbed by everyone in the class. Such is rarely the case. In real life teaching situations, one is likely to be faced with a room full of children of widely varying ability. Some will relish writing, and others will abhor it. Some will gleefully experiment with new techniques, while others prefer to stick with what they already know. How can a teacher effectively instruct such a diverse group?

Differentiated instruction is the answer. By teaching one lesson and assigning different tasks based upon student ability, you can reach and engage both the advanced and reluctant writers in your classroom. It all begins with Target Skills.

TARGET SKILLS: ORGANIZATIONAL SKILLS, COMPOSING SKILLS, AND CONVENTION SKILLS

Target Skills are the basic writing skills that all proficient writers need to know and use. The Target Skill lessons in the book are designed to give young writers explicit instruction in writer's craft. There are three types of Target Skills:

- Organizational Target Skills. These are the skills that writers use to construct their writing pieces. They include topic selection, opening and ending techniques, paragraphs, supporting details, and transitions.
- Composing Target Skills. These are the literary skills and conventions that add style and voice to student writing. These include creating characters, setting the mood, using imagery, making effective word choices, and many more.
- Convention Target Skills. These deal mostly with the conventions of writing, namely grammar, punctuation, spelling, and usage.

The major focus of this book is on the first two types of Target Skills, organizational and composing. These are effectively taught using the WHAM mini-lesson format explained in the next section.

You can also teach conventions using this approach by explicitly modeling the skill in your mini-lesson and asking students to apply the skill as part of their revision process.

THE WHAM (WATCH, HELP, APPLY, MASTER) MINI-LESSON FORMAT

The mini-lessons in this book follow what I have termed the WHAM format, an easy-to-remember acronym for Watch, Help, Apply, and Master. This four-step model gives students an increasing amount of involvement and independence in acquiring a skill. At first, students *watch* the teacher demonstrate a skill. They are then asked to *help* the teacher apply the skill to a given example. From there, they *apply* the skill independently by practicing examples on their own. Finally, after the teacher assesses the level of competence displayed, students learn to *master* the skill in a differentiated workstation geared to their particular level. Students may advance as they accomplish each workstation task successfully.

The WHAM format echoes the "I do, you watch" gradual release of responsibility model advanced by Jeffrey Wilhelm in his book *Strategic Reading* (Heinemann, 2001). It adds the advantage of creating terminology that teachers and students can share; when I tell students we're going to "WHAM" a skill, they know the steps we are going to take.

Each mini-lesson should last from ten to fifteen minutes. Ideally, each part of the process should last for about three or four minutes. Of course, if you are introducing a new skill to students, you may have to spend more time modeling the skill early in the mini-lesson. For skills that are mostly review or practice, you may wish to adjust your timing for less modeling and more application of the skill.

Given such a brief amount of time, it is essential that both teachers and students clearly understand their roles during each step of the process. I find that using the term "WHAM" with students assists them in becoming familiar with the format and understanding what is expected of them at each stage of the lesson.

Here are the steps and roles involved in the WHAM process.

Step	Teacher's Role	Student's Role
WATCH	Demonstrate the skill	Watch the teacher demonstrate the skill
HELP	Assist students in understanding the skill	"Help" the teacher to apply the skill demonstrated
APPLY	Check understanding; assist students who are struggling; review responses	Apply the new skill to teacher-assigned examples
MASTER	Facilitate group work; assign differentiated tasks to groups; conference with students	Practice the skill independently; incorporate the skill into a draft or writing notebook assignment

I find that it takes students only a few days to become comfortable with this format and the roles they will assume. Using the format on a consistent basis is the key to success. Students actually begin to anticipate the next step in the lesson and may want to jump ahead!

The WHAM format works because it is based on a number of sound educational principles.

- **Clear roles and expectations.** Students can learn their roles in the process quickly and understand what is expected of them at each stage of the writing process.
- **Predictability.** Students know that lessons will follow the format each day and therefore feel comfortable with the process.
- **Structured approach.** Lessons begin with teacher instruction, but each step increases the amount of student independence in the process. This gives teachers and students the opportunity to check understanding at each stage of the process.
- **Scaffolding of skills.** Each task builds on the last, and mini-lessons may build upon skills taught in earlier workshops.
- **Modeling of skills.** Ordinary writing is often shown in contrast with improved or exceptional writing. These examples help students identify weaknesses and strengths in their own writing.
- **Accountability.** Students are accountable for the mini-lesson itself, application of the skill in their writing notebooks, completion of workstation tasks and, eventually, incorporation of the skill into a graded completed work.

The *master* part of the mini-lesson is when students are put to work in their differentiated workstations.

ASSIGNING DIFFERENTIATED WORKSTATION TASKS

Some schools call them *workstations*. Others refer to them as *writing circles, writing stations, writing groups*, or simply *group work*. Whatever the name, workstations are places where students write. Writing takes place in a group setting and concludes with some type of presentation of the day's work.

In my own experience with groups of thirty or more students (and hence seven to eight groups of four students each) of varying degrees of competence, assigning appropriate tasks became a dizzying challenge. Even in whole-group instruction, where all students work on the skill taught in the mini-lesson, it is apparent that different groups "get" the mini-lesson to a greater or lesser extent and that a single workstation task is inadequate. In small-group instruction, where each group may be practicing a different (but needed) skill, assigning appropriate work is especially daunting. The differentiated workstations in this book help solve these difficulties and let you, the teacher, focus on your most important work—assisting students in their journeys to become competent writers.

As the name implies, differentiated workstations attempt to match tasks to the levels of the various groups in your workshop. Groups can then work at their level of competency, avoiding frustration and allowing students to master skills as they proceed from easier tasks to more challenging work.

Because not all students in a class need work on the same skills, you can assign different writer's-craft tasks to different groups. For example, if two groups have mastered similes, you can move them on to metaphor workstation tasks while your other groups continue practicing similes. Given the large number of tasks in this book—more than 200—you can get as sophisticated as you like in your groupings and assignments.

Each mini-lesson is accompanied by four workstation tasks, Tasks A through D. While some of these tasks are genre specific, most are arranged in order of difficulty, with Task A being the easiest. Students who are having problems understanding or applying the Target Skill can begin with Task A and work their way to Task D.

To keep your job as simple as possible, there are a number of ways to assign appropriate tasks to student writers. These include:

- Baseline essays. This book contains a chapter on each basic writing strand (reports, how-to essays, persuasive essays, narratives, and literary responses). Within each of these chapters is a sample task and rubric that may be used as a baseline essay at the beginning of the school year.

- Assessment of mini-lesson proficiency. When using the WHAM lesson format, you can assess student understanding of the Target Skill during the apply part of the lesson. This allows you to form "on-the-fly" groups based upon your observation of actual student work. This method is especially helpful when a new Target Skill is being taught for which there is no baseline assessment.

- Conferencing notes. During writing time, you can conference with your students to gauge their level of proficiency and assign tasks accordingly.

- Class evaluation sheets. Following the completion of a major assignment, you can fill out a class evaluation sheet like the one in the **Teaching Resources** section in this book. This assessment tool can give you a visual snapshot of the proficiency of your class at the various Target Skill mini-lessons you have taught and act as a guidepost for future differentiated task assignments. See the **Teaching Resources** section at the end of this book for more information and a blank class evaluation sheet template.

- Workstation progress chart. This chart, located in the **Teaching Resources** section, can be given to each student for inclusion in the writing notebook to track his or her own progress. Students can use it to request assignment to skills they wish to practice, and teachers can use it as an "at a glance" reference to discover tasks that need additional work. See the **Teaching Resources** section for more information and a blank chart for duplication.

If you're new to differentiated instruction, you may wish to start slowly by teaching whole-class mini-lessons for the majority of the class and creating a single small group consisting of students who need explicit instruction in one of the Target Skills. As you become more familiar with this process, you can add more small groups or even allow students to choose their own workstations as they learn to identify skills that need reinforcement. Whatever you do, make sure your choice works for you. If it does, excellent instruction is sure to be the outcome.

Setting up Your Writer's Workshop

There are probably as many variations on how to set up a writing workshop as there are teachers. Yet there are certain characteristics that are common to most successful workshops and some techniques that will enhance your experience in implementing the lessons in this book into your own workshop.

ESTABLISHING ROUTINES

One key aspect of setting up your writer's workshop for success is making sure that students know that this time is for writing and writing alone. Any reading or research needed for the day's writing should already have been completed. For language arts teachers, this is usually readily accomplished by designating certain periods of the week as reading periods and the rest as writing periods. In many schools, language arts classes are already set up as double blocks of time which may be split between reading and writing lessons.

Other subject areas, however, generally do not designate entire periods as writing periods. If your department does not, simply take a do-it-yourself approach and devote a few periods of time to writer's workshop when you're asking students to produce a major writing piece. The time students spend analyzing, synthesizing, and retelling information deepens their understanding of the subject area and, in the end, produces far better written work.

If you're new to teaching writing, start with the basics. Establish routines for the distribution of any materials your students might need for the day at the beginning of each period. Then allocate time for your mini-lesson, student work time, and a closing in which students present the day's work to the class or to a partner or group.

If you teach in a team or house, it is preferable for every teacher on the team to approach writer's workshop in a similar manner. While there's no need for a lockstep approach, some consistency among the subject areas simplifies the process for students and teachers alike. Discuss with your team which routines are best for your student population.

THE WRITING NOTEBOOK

A writing notebook can be a powerful tool for students and teachers. Just as it is important for students to have a designated time to write, it is equally important for them to have a designated place to actually record their writing. Whether it's in a composition book or a writing section in their binder, keeping student writing in one place facilitates organization and creates a resource that students can refer to when needed.

The easiest way to organize the notebook is to create a table of contents in which students record the date, lesson, and page number where each day's work can be found. If you teach leads in September and a student needs to revisit that topic in May, he or she can easily find the lesson by referring back to the contents of the notebook.

Many teachers keep it simple with just a table of contents and work pages, but you can add features to writer's notebooks if you prefer. Some teachers add spelling and vocabulary sections, to-do lists for unfinished assignments, a section for grammar and usage, and so on. If you're new to writer's workshop, err on the side of simplicity; you can always add features to the notebook in the future if you decide you need them.

You may want to give each student a copy of the workstation progress checklist found in the **Teaching Resources** section and have them staple it in their notebook. You can use this to chart student progress.

Students should be encouraged to pick works they wish to draft from their notebooks. When students have mastered a Target Skill in their notebooks, they should apply those skills to their drafts. It is helpful for students to have a draft folder separate from their writing notebook. You may also want to keep a folder for each child to store their finished writing pieces.

SAMPLE LESSON WALK-THROUGH

As a middle-school language arts teacher, I have students come to me for forty-five- or ninety-minute blocks of instruction and move on to the next subject class at the conclusion. At the beginning of each block, writer's notebooks and draft folders are distributed, along with any other materials that may be needed that day, such as sticky notes, highlighters, etc. As soon as everyone is settled and ready to work, the mini-lesson begins.

The process is essentially the same if teaching a subject area other than language arts, but you may wish to confer with your students' language arts teacher to see whether there are any procedures in place that you might want to mimic in your own writer's workshop. Consistency is key; it lessens confusion when students understand that the rules for writing are the same in all their subject areas.

I often use the lessons exactly as you see them in this book by placing them on an overhead. You may do this as well; of course, you are free to use the lessons here in any manner you choose, including linking them to whatever reading is taking place in your classroom. While any and all of these mini-lessons are suitable for whole-class instruction, they may be revisited and re-taught to smaller groups when the need becomes apparent.

The *watch* portion of the mini-lesson is arguably the most important. It begins with an explanation of the skill to be mastered that day and then moves into teacher-directed modeling of the skill. All of the lessons in this book include an example for teachers to explain as the students watch. It is important, however, to use outside examples whenever possible, either instead of or in addition to the overhead example. Read-alouds are a good source of such material and give students a real world example written by a skilled author with whom they are familiar. Another great source is student-generated writing. What better way to teach metaphors, for example, than showing an excellent example penned by a member of the class? This not only celebrates student success, but also conveys the idea that the skill can be expertly executed by nonprofessional writers as well.

The examples accompanying each lesson in this book frequently contain an *original* and a *revised* example. The *original* examples attempt, as much as possible, to mimic actual student writing, and the *revised* examples show how the writing might look when the skill is applied. Teacher-led explanation of why the revised version is superior helps cement the importance of the skill in the students' minds. Here's an example of the watch portion from the mini-lesson, "Showing through Dialogue."

WATCH how it's done.

ORIGINAL SENTENCE:

Regina was disappointed.

REVISED SENTENCE, SHOWING CHARACTER THROUGH DIALOGUE:

"I don't believe it!" Regina cried. "All that work for nothing! I never wanted anything more in my life, and now it's over!"

The next component of the WHAM mini-lesson is *help*. This part is still teacher directed but asks for student input, thus increasing student responsibility and engagement. The teacher presents another original example and asks for help in applying the new skill to it. This is a time for student participation. Consider the following *help* example.

HELP with this sentence:

Chester was overjoyed.

The teacher asks students how this ordinary sentence could be converted into dialogue. If a student volunteers a **telling** piece of dialogue, such as *Chester said, "I'm happy,"* the teacher may either point out that the line does not **show** though dialogue or ask for student opinion on whether the line accomplishes the skill. The latter method is preferable as it gives students an opportunity to discuss their understanding of the application of the skill. When a student volunteer gives an appropriate example, the teacher writes it on the overhead (blank lines are provided in this book's mini-lessons for this purpose) and asks if anyone can add to it. Eventually the class will, with the teacher's assistance, create a solid example of the skill together. This sort of collaborative work not only reinforces the skill, but models the group effort that students will need to engage in when they go to their workstations.

At this point, the teacher may field questions on the application of the skill. Once issues are resolved, the class moves on to the next part of the mini-lesson.

The *apply* component moves students toward even greater independence. At this stage, students are given a task to accomplish in their notebooks. For example, the *apply* portion of the "Showing through Dialogue" mini-lesson looks like this:

APPLY   this skill in your writing notebook. Change each sentence below into dialogue that shows what the character is feeling.

---

1. My dad was confused.
2. Arthur was hungry.
3. Mimi couldn't believe what she heard.
4. Simon was irritated at his mom.
5. My sister was caring.

Students work on a limited number of examples to demonstrate that they have understood the skill well enough to apply it on their own. While students are working, the teacher has the opportunity to check with each group and assist with any problems or clarify what needs to be done. At the conclusion of work time, which may last from five to ten minutes, the teacher will review student responses to the task with the whole group.

During the *apply* time, the teacher may evaluate student understanding and decide which workstation task to assign to each group. Once the students know what their assigned task is, the mini-lesson concludes and work on the *master* portion of the lesson, which includes differentiated workstation tasks, begins.

Allocate a set time for completion of tasks to help keep students focused. Fifteen to twenty minutes should be sufficient for most students and most tasks. You may use this work time to conference with students and to plan future workstations based upon your conferences.

Students should share their work to conclude the day's lesson. Closings can include author's chair readings or "group shares" within each group. However you close, your closing should help students reflect on the day's work through positive feedback and reinforcement.

Repeat this process 180 or so times, and you should end up with a productive year of writing!

Writing a Report

ELEMENTS OF REPORT WRITING

Reports are the most basic form of informational writing for students. Generally, a writer's task in a report is to conduct research, distill the salient points, and present them in an appropriate form for the intended audience. This can be a more daunting task than it first seems for young writers.

Reports begin with an introduction that states the topic and gives some indication of the type of information to follow. The body consists of research written in support of the topic, and the conclusion summarizes the discussion. Charts, graphs, polls, surveys, pictures, and sidebars are often used to help explain the information gathered.

THE CHALLENGES OF REPORT WRITING

Challenge #1: Finding appropriate topics. You want to focus on topics that will enhance learning. Your student writers want to report on subjects they are interested in. Often, the only way to strike a balance is to spend significant time allowing students to explore the myriad topics from which they may choose.
Solution. Teach the mini-lesson "Finding Topics: Reports" on page 46. Proceed to the workstations, and allow all your students to begin with Task A, which encourages them to brainstorm ideas. Work students through the progression of tasks until they have refined their topics to meet your educational goals.

Challenge #2: Viewing reports as evaluative tools. Too frequently, writing a report is used only as an evaluative tool—the culminating activity of a unit that's already been learned. That's a shame because the writing process is a wonderful learning opportunity in itself. Getting students to think about how they would present the information as they learn it engages them in deeper thinking about their topics.
Solution. Start the writing process early, and refer to it frequently. As soon as students begin narrowing down topics, they should begin their research. Teach the mini-lesson "Writing the Body: The Five Ws of Non-fiction" on page 108 and the related workstations to demonstrate how their learning will be incorporated into their writing.

Challenge #3: Keeping it interesting. Informational reports can become a snooze quickly if students merely present fact after fact. While you can teach interesting leads and conclusions, the body is a greater challenge. Of course, sidebars and graphics can help, but student writers also need to know how to make their sentences livelier.

Solution. Mix in composing Target Skills. Teaching some or all of the "Word Choice" mini-lessons in **Chapter 10—Composing Techniques: Target Skill Lessons and Workstation Tasks** will make student writing more varied and interesting. In addition, the "Revision" mini-lessons will show your students how to vary their sentences.

CHOOSING LESSONS TO TEACH

The task and rubric at the end of this chapter may be reproduced and given to students as is, or you may modify them to meet the needs of your class. You should introduce the task only after you have completed the first two lessons in the following list to ensure that your students have an adequate enough understanding of topic choice to begin writing. Students will also need to have much of their research completed before progressing to the writing stage.

The task is simple enough to be used as a baseline writing assignment at the beginning of the year to assist you in determining proper student placement in workstations. To ensure success, you should teach the following mini-lessons (at a minimum) to cover the skills asked for in the task:

- Finding Topics: Reports . . . 46
- Finding Topics: Narrowing Your Focus . . . 56
- Beginning Techniques: Lead Types—Interesting Facts, Quotations, and Anecdotes . . . 64
- Writing the Body: The Five Ws of Non-fiction . . . 108
- Creating Paragraphs: Topic Sentences . . . 68
- Creating Paragraphs: Supporting Details . . . 70
- Revision: Sentence Variety . . . 156
- Revision: Edit the Excess . . . 158
- Ending Techniques: Ending Types—Restate the Main Idea, Make a Recommendation, and Make a Prediction . . . 82

Please note that these mini-lessons and workstations are the minimum necessary to teach what is asked of students on the task. Additional mini-lessons and workstation tasks can be taught as needed. Refer to page 161 in the **Teaching Resources** section for a full list of skill lessons that apply to writing reports.

BUILDING STYLE INTO REPORTS

Reports tend to be dry and boring unless you take the time to show your students how to punch up these informational writings. Here are some lessons you can teach in addition to the basic skills that will help develop your students' style and make their work shine!

Teach point of view. If the report is about famous people, why not have students give their report from the point of view of that person? If the report is about a place, have students create a fictional character through whose eyes the reader can visualize the place. The lessons on point of view in this book can help you teach this important writing skill.

Teach tableau. Freezing a moment in history or in a person's life is an excellent way to breathe life into a report, and it also gets students thinking about the importance of each person and event they're reporting on as they decide which to choose for their tableau.

Teach flashbacks. Because many reports deal with people and places in history, teaching your students to use flashbacks can be an effective technique in helping them relate the events of their topic to modern-day events.

WRITING REPORTS ACROSS THE CURRICULUM

The beauty of reports is their versatility. No matter what the subject area, students can report on the people, places, and events that relate to the specific curriculum you are teaching.

The content of reports won't vary widely from student to student because the facts are fixed. To make reports relevant to your subject area, focus instead on the writing skills your students need to add their unique voice to the topic.

USING THE TASK AND RUBRIC FOR WRITING A REPORT

The following pages contain a reproducible task and rubric. Give a copy of the task to each student before drafting begins. This sets the expectations for the writing piece. The rubric should be used to score student writing after drafting is completed and will let both you and your students know what areas need additional revision.

Task for a Report

After exploring potential topics for your report, choose one that you feel interested in. Research your topic to make sure you have enough material to report on. Follow the guidelines below.

In your report, be sure to:

☐ Introduce your report with an interesting fact, quotation, or a bold statement. Your introduction should make the reader want to read on.

☐ Write paragraphs with clear topic sentences and support them with specific details and/or ideas.

☐ Include the five Ws of non-fiction to be sure you have fully explored your topic.

☐ Use varied sentence length to keep your writing interesting.

☐ Leave out unnecessary or inaccurate details.

☐ Conclude by restating the main idea, making a recommendation for further action, or by making a prediction about what will happen if your advice is not followed.

Remember to check your paper for correct spelling, grammar, punctuation, and paragraphing.

Rubric for a Report

4: OUTSTANDING	3: GOOD	2: NEEDS IMPROVEMENT	1: NOT DONE
Begin with an interesting fact, a quotation, or a bold statement that makes the reader want to read on?			
Engages with an original, interesting fact, quotation, or bold statement that grabs the reader's attention and makes him/her want to read on.	Engages with an interesting fact, quotation, or bold statement. The reader wants to read on.	Introduction needs improvement and/or the technique used doesn't quite make the reader feel compelled to read on.	Little attempt to engage the reader and/or the reader has no reason to read on.
Include paragraphs with clear topic sentences and support them with specific details and/or ideas?			
Each paragraph has a clear topic sentence that is well supported and reinforces the topic as a whole.	Topic sentences are generally clear and supported by details and ideas.	Topic sentences may be unclear at times and/or may not always have adequate support.	Topic sentences are confusing or missing. Support for topics is weak or missing.
Include the five Ws of non-fiction writing?			
Uses the five Ws to effectively discuss the facts of the topic.	Uses the five Ws to discuss the facts of the topic.	The five Ws may need to be more clearly discussed.	Some or all of the five Ws are missing.
Use varied sentence length to keep your writing interesting?			
Excellent mix of short and longer sentences that keep the writing crisp and interesting.	Good mix of short and longer sentences that keep the writing interesting.	Attempt made at varying sentence length, but more revision is needed to keep reader interest.	Most sentences are about the same length.
Leave out unnecessary or inaccurate details?			
All details are necessary to understanding the topic. They are interesting and accurate.	Most details are necessary to understanding the topic. They are mostly interesting and accurate.	Some details may be unnecessary and/or inaccurate.	Contains unnecessary or inaccurate details that confuse the reader.
Conclude by restating the main idea, making a recommendation, or making a prediction?			
Effectively concludes and leaves the reader with something to think about.	Concludes well and gives the reader a general summary of the topic.	Has some sense of closure but the closing technique needs work.	Gives little or no sense of closure and/or does not use a closing technique.

COMMENTS:

5

Writing a Persuasive Essay

ELEMENTS OF PERSUASIVE ESSAYS

Elementary-school writers are usually taught the opinion piece, which is the precursor to the persuasive essay. Generally, the opinion piece asks only that the writer state his or her opinion and support it with evidence. The persuasive essay goes a very difficult step further as it seeks to change the mind of the reader. This step is challenging because student writers must place themselves in the minds of their readers to anticipate questions and counterarguments.

You can get as fancy as you want in your tasks, asking students to provide charts, tables, bibliographies, illustrations, captions, sidebars, and so forth, but a good persuasive essay itself generally boils down to an engaging introduction and conclusion that frame well-crafted arguments.

THE CHALLENGES OF PERSUASIVE WRITING

Challenge #1: Finding topics to debate. It seems obvious to adult writers, but the first essential element of a persuasive piece is that the subject be debatable. Students frequently gravitate to topics that really aren't persuasive topics at all. One cannot debate how many prisoners are on death row in America, but you can debate whether they should be executed. Likewise, topics that present only one strong side offer little opportunity for persuasion. Saying that we need cleaner parks isn't a good topic because most people agree. Arguing how to pay for cleaner parks will spark debate.

Solution. Provide explicit instruction in finding debatable topics. The best way for student writers to find topics is to brainstorm issues that have two strong sides to them. Teach the mini-lesson "Finding Topics: Persuasive Essays" to get your students thinking about the issues they might want to address.

Challenge #2: Understanding both sides of the issue. Student writers often pick topics that they believe in passionately, which makes it difficult to see that there is another side to the issue. For example, they may believe that they have a right to play violent video games that they see as harmless. They may not understand (or wish to hear) that adults may have a valid difference of opinion that needs to be addressed.

Solution. Have students argue the other side. I've often required students to argue their opponent's side of the issue prior to approving their topics. Not only does this show their genuine interest in the topic, but more importantly, it gets them to consider the points they will need to address to be truly persuasive.

Challenge #3: Not addressing reader's concerns. Even after arguing the other side, many students fail to discuss it in their essays, thinking they are more persuasive arguing their own side only. Convincing them to include opposing arguments can be a challenge.

Solution. Model effective persuasive essays to show students how to address readers' concerns without weakening their own arguments. Op-ed pieces can be especially effective in modeling this technique.

CHOOSING LESSONS TO TEACH

The task and rubric at the end of this chapter may be reproduced and given to students as is, or you may modify them to meet the needs of your class. The task is simple enough to be used as a baseline writing assignment at the beginning of the year to assist you in determining proper student placement in workstations. To ensure success, you should teach the following mini-lessons (at a minimum) to cover the skills asked for in the task:

- Finding Topics: Persuasive Essays . . . 48
- Finding Topics: Narrowing Your Focus . . . 56
- Beginning Techniques: Lead Types—Interesting Facts, Quotations, and Anecdotes . . . 64
- Beginning Techniques: Lead Types—Questions, Descriptions, and Bold Statements (focus on bold statements) . . . 66
- Writing the Body: The Five Ws of Non-fiction . . . 108
- Creating Paragraphs: Topic Sentences . . . 68
- Creating Paragraphs: Supporting Details . . . 70
- Word Choice: Choosing Strong Words . . . 124
- Ending Techniques: Ending Types—Restate the Main Idea, Make a Recommendation, and Make a Prediction . . . 82

Please note that these mini-lessons and workstations are the minimum necessary to teach what is asked of students on the task. Additional mini-lessons and workstation tasks can be taught as needed. Refer to page 162 in the **Teaching Resources** section for a full list of skill lessons that apply to writing persuasive essays.

BUILDING STYLE INTO PERSUASIVE ESSAYS

There are many ways of bringing your students' own individual style into their persuasive writing. The following lessons will help put a stamp of individuality on your students' persuasive pieces.

Teach compare/contrast. One of the challenges of persuasive essays is showing students how to compare two different scenarios, the for and against. Teaching them to effectively compare and contrast will help them meet this challenge.

Teach adverbs. Using strong adverbs greatly enhances any persuasive argument. Teaching the "Word Choice: Adding Adverbs" mini-lesson on page 130 will show your students the power of choosing effective adverbs for their writing.

Teach sensory details. If students can make the reader experience, through the senses, the negative effects of the *against* position of their argument or the positive effects of the *for* position, they will have gone a long way toward convincing their reader. As a side benefit, sensory description greatly enhances the writing itself and helps engage the reader.

WRITING PERSUASIVE ESSAYS ACROSS THE CURRICULUM

Persuasive writing has traditionally been done mostly in social studies classes. Here are some ideas to help you implement persuasive writing across the curriculum.

Language arts. Have students discuss what their next author or genre study should be. I often ask students to write persuasive proposal letters before starting a new study. These can be developed into full essays if desired.

Science. Ask students to decide which areas of science deserve the biggest increase in funding. Should we devote a larger share of limited resources to space exploration, meteorology, the environment, or looking for cures for diseases? Students can make a choice and argue why their choice deserves an increase in funding more than other areas.

Math. Ask students to persuade you why they should/should not be allowed to use calculators on tests.

Music, art, chorus, technology, physical education. Have students persuade the principal that more periods per week should be devoted to these courses.

USING THE TASK AND RUBRIC FOR WRITING A PERSUASIVE ESSAY

The following pages contain a reproducible task and rubric. Give a copy of the task to each student before drafting begins. This sets the expectations for the writing piece. The rubric should be used to score student writing after drafting is completed and will let both you and your students know what areas need additional revision.

Task for a Persuasive Essay

After examining topics for your persuasive essay, choose one that you feel strongly about as your topic. Make sure you understand both sides of the issue before your begin drafting.

In your persuasive essay, be sure to:

☐ Introduce your essay with an interesting fact, a quotation, or a bold statement. Follow up by stating your three main arguments in the opening paragraph.

☐ Present each of your three main arguments in a separate paragraph. Support each argument with specific details and/or ideas.

☐ Include the five Ws of non-fiction to be sure you have fully explained your issue.

☐ Address possible reader concerns, questions, and counterarguments.

☐ Use strong words to help convince your reader.

☐ Leave out unnecessary or inaccurate details.

☐ Conclude by answering the question you asked in the introduction. (For example, *Now you can see that with the proper materials and a little patience, just about anyone can build a model airplane from materials they can find in their home.*)

Remember to check your paper for correct spelling, grammar, punctuation, and paragraphing.

Rubric for a Persuasive Essay

4: OUTSTANDING	3: GOOD	2: NEEDS IMPROVEMENT	1: NOT DONE
Begin with an engaging introduction that includes a statement of your major arguments?			
Engages by making the reader truly think about the topic and clearly lists the major arguments that will be made.	Engages the reader in the topic and lists the arguments that will be made.	Introduction needs improvement and/or doesn't clearly discuss the arguments that will be made.	Little attempt to engage the reader and/or no discussion of the arguments that will be made.
Present each argument in a separate paragraph and support each argument?			
Each argument is presented in a separate paragraph that is well supported and reinforces the persuasive argument as a whole.	Each argument is presented in a separate paragraph that is well supported.	Arguments wander somewhat and/or need additional support.	Arguments are presented in a confusing manner and/or lack any meaningful support.
Include the five Ws of non-fiction writing?			
Uses the five Ws to effectively discuss the facts of the topic.	Uses the five Ws to discuss the facts of the topic.	The five Ws are generally present and clear.	Some or all of the five Ws are missing.
Use strong words to persuade the reader?			
Uses strong words that give the reader a sense of the importance of the issue and help to persuade.	Often uses strong words that help create a sense of the importance of the issue. These words help to persuade.	Sometimes uses strong words that help create a sense of the importance of the issue and help to persuade.	Few, if any, strong word choices.
Leave out unnecessary or inaccurate details?			
All details are necessary and accurate. Details support the arguments made.	Most details are necessary and accurate. Mostly support the arguments made.	Some details may be unnecessary and /or inaccurate.	Contains unnecessary or inaccurate details that confuse the reader.
Conclude by restating the main idea, making a recommendation, or making a prediction?			
Effectively concludes and leaves the reader with something to think about.	Concludes well and gives the reader a general summary of the arguments made.	Has some sense of closure but the closing technique needs work.	Gives little or no sense of closure and does not use a closing technique.

COMMENTS:

Writing a How-to (Procedural) Essay

ELEMENTS OF A HOW-TO ESSAY

How-to essays, also called procedural essays, are amazingly versatile and can be used virtually anywhere in the curriculum. They are easily adapted to science and math, and they are a great vehicle to foster student writing in those subject areas.

Most how-to essays consist of a number of written steps sandwiched between the introduction and conclusion. They may contain other parts, such as student advice to the reader, various sidebars with extra information, diagrams, or captioned pictures. Whatever extras you include, the basic formula usually remains the same.

A how-to essay generally seems pretty straightforward, because its purpose is so clear: to instruct the reader in how to do some task. Students quickly learn, however, that how-to writing is littered with "gotchas" that can interfere with reader understanding. Teaching a few skills can greatly improve the clarity of student writing in this genre as well as foster a greater understanding of the subject by the writer as he or she ponders how to explain the task to a novice.

THE CHALLENGES OF HOW-TO WRITING

Challenge #1: Finding narrow topics. Student writers naturally choose topics that they know well when writing how-to essays. The trouble begins when they choose a topic they know so well that they end up trying to explain every facet of the topic to the reader. A student who loves basketball may try to explain the whole game, which is obviously impossible. Choosing a narrower topic, such as "How to shoot a free throw" is more manageable and keeps the writer focused.
Solution: Provide explicit instruction in narrowing topics. The only way to get students to narrow their topics is to show them how. Demonstrate some unwieldy topics for them, and model how to pluck narrower topics from them. Do the mini-lesson on "Finding Topics: Narrowing Your Focus," and assign workstations as appropriate. After drafts are completed, you should teach the mini-lesson "Revision: Edit the Excess" to ensure that students have kept their writing as narrow as their topics.

Challenge #2: Lack of specificity. Since they are generally intimately familiar with their own topics, student writers often descend into generalities when giving instructions. Overuse of pronouns rather than specific nouns is a particular impediment to clarity for young writers. Solution: Emphasize specificity in word choice. Teach students to use specific nouns in their how-to writing. Do the mini-lesson "Word Choice: Using Specific Nouns," and assign workstations as appropriate. As an adjunct, you may also wish to teach "Word Choice: Choosing Strong Words" to encourage students to think about word choice as they strive for clarity in their essays.

Challenge #3: Clarifying time and order. In any sort of procedural writing, giving the reader a sense of the time needed to complete the task and the proper order of the task is critical. As students work on creating an organizing structure for their essay, transitional terms help them stay focused on both time and order.
Solution: Teaching transitional phrases. Getting students to express themselves with words like next, then, an hour later, etc., focuses them on the proper order of the steps of their how-to and can give a sense of time needed to accomplish the task. Teach the mini-lesson "Creating Paragraphs: Time Transitions," and have students practice this skill in the accompanying workstations before applying it to their own writing.

CHOOSING LESSONS TO TEACH

The task and rubric at the end of this chapter may be reproduced and given to students as is, or you may modify them to meet the needs of your class. The task is simple enough to be used as a baseline writing assignment at the beginning of the year to assist you in determining proper student placement in workstations. To ensure success, you should teach the following mini-lessons (at a minimum) to cover the skills asked for in the task.

Please note that these mini-lessons and workstations are the minimum necessary to teach what is asked of students on the task. Additional mini-lessons and workstation tasks can be taught as needed. Refer to page 163 in the **Teaching Resources** section for a full list of skill lessons that apply to writing how-to essays.

BUILDING STYLE INTO HOW-TO ESSAYS

Teaching these additional lessons will add pizzazz to any procedural piece.

Teach tableau. You can have students use tableau to describe the scenario the reader might find himself in when he realizes he needs to learn how to do something. For example, a how-to on changing a tire might include a tableau of a driver at the moment he hears the dreadful pop as he drives on a lonely highway on a cold night, realizing he doesn't know how to change a tire.

Teach hyperbole. While students need to be precise in their instruction in a how-to, it's perfectly acceptable for them to exaggerate the ease of the proposed task, or better yet, the difficulties the reader will face by not following the steps precisely. This can also add a touch of humor to how-to essays.

Teach sentence variety. How-to essays often get bogged down in repetition of words as students refer back to specific parts or steps of the process. Teaching them sentence variety makes writing crisper.

WRITING HOW-TO ESSAYS ACROSS THE CURRICULUM

Since every subject area instructs in something, how-to essays naturally lend themselves to implementation across the curriculum. Planning a special "How-to Week" in your school is a great way to generate writing school-wide. The ideas are really limitless, but here are some to get teachers started in almost all subject areas.

Language arts

- Write a poem
- Write a letter
- Select a good book
- Create a storyboard

Social studies

- Make a bill into law
- Vote in an election
- Read a map
- Determine longitude and latitude
- Study a civilization

Math

- Multiply two-digit numbers
- Find the hypotenuse
- Draw polynomials
- Calculate a restaurant tip
- Calculate sales tax

Science

- Use the scientific method
- Use a microscope
- Read the periodic table of elements
- Stargaze
- Predict the weather

Art

- Draw a cartoon character
- Make a papier-mâché mask
- Make a loom
- Create pottery
- Draw a self-portrait

Foreign language

- Conjugate a verb
- Order from a restaurant in a foreign language
- Learn a new language
- Exchange foreign currency

Technology

- Build a webpage
- Replace a hard drive
- Add memory to a computer
- Use a word processor
- Make your computer secure

Physical education

- Throw a football
- Referee a game
- Show good sportsmanship
- Form a good team
- Get physically fit

Music

- Read music
- Choose a musical instrument
- Form a band
- Make a percussion instrument
- Tune an instrument

USING THE TASK AND RUBRIC FOR WRITING A HOW-TO ESSAY

The following pages contain a reproducible task and rubric. Give a copy of the task to each student before drafting begins. This sets the expectations for the writing piece. The rubric should be used to score student writing after drafting is completed and will let both you and your students know what areas need additional revision.

Task for a How-to Essay

Write about something that you know how to do very well. Write a how-to essay on that subject, explaining to a novice reader the exact steps he or she must follow.

In your how-to essay, be sure to:

☐ Introduce your essay with a question that engages the reader and makes him/her want to explore your topic further. (For example, "Do you have what it takes to build a model airplane from scratch?")

☐ Explain why the reader might want to do this task.

☐ Explain the task as a series of steps to be followed in order.

☐ Discuss any special materials that might be needed.

☐ Use transitional words to help explain the steps.

☐ Leave out unnecessary or inaccurate details.

☐ Use specific nouns to help you explain each step.

☐ Conclude by answering the question you asked in the introduction. (For example, "Now you can see that with the proper materials and a little patience, just about anyone can build a model airplane from materials they can find in their home.")

Remember to check your paper for correct spelling, grammar, punctuation, and paragraphing.

Rubric for a How-to Essay

4: OUTSTANDING	3: GOOD	2: NEEDS IMPROVEMENT	1: NOT DONE
Begin by asking a question that engages the reader in your topic?			
Asks a thought-provoking question that immediately engages the reader.	Asks a question that engages the reader in the topic.	Asks a question, but the question is general and/or does not help engage the reader in the topic.	No attempt to ask a question. Reader is not engaged by the introduction.
Explain the task as a series of steps to be followed in order?			
Explains the task clearly and thoughtfully, leaving no questions in the reader's mind.	Explains the task, leaving few questions in the reader's mind about how to accomplish the task.	Attempts to explain the task, but the reader may have difficulty following the order or understanding the time sequence.	Explanation is out of order or difficult for the reader to follow.
Discuss any special materials that might be needed?			
Discusses the materials needed in a sidebar that is easily understood and referenced in the text.	Discusses the materials needed and how they will be used.	Discusses some of the materials needed, but type or amount may be unclear.	Materials not discussed, or discussion is confusing to the reader.
Use transitional words to help the reader understand the process?			
Uses appropriate transitional words that give the reader a sense of the order and time needed to accomplish each step.	Often uses appropriate transitional words that help the reader understand the process.	Some transitional words used, but more are needed to help the reader understand the order and/or time needed to complete the task.	Transitional words not used or used incorrectly.
Leave out unnecessary or inaccurate details?			
All details are necessary and accurate.	Most details are necessary and accurate.	Some details may be unnecessary and/or inaccurate.	Contains unnecessary or inaccurate details that confuse the reader.
Conclude by answering the question posed in the introduction?			
Answers the question and creates a satisfying sense of closure.	Answers the question and creates a sense of closure.	Answers the question but doesn't give a sense of closure to the writing.	Doesn't answer the question or bring a sense of closure to the writing.

COMMENTS:

Writing a Narrative

ELEMENTS OF A NARRATIVE

A narrative, in the simplest terms, is a sequence of events told by a narrator. It may be fiction or non-fiction. It should contain, at a minimum, a setting, a plot, characters, a conflict, and dialogue.

Even though most of the narratives children read are fictional, most of the stories they write are personal-experience narratives. While these are a good place for middle-schoolers to start, it is important for them to transition toward writing fictional narratives as they develop as writers. Writing fictional narratives challenges writers to think through the entire writing process in a way that is unmatched by a mere retelling of actual events.

THE CHALLENGES OF NARRATIVE WRITING

Challenge #1: Lack of experience. Let's face it. Even as adults, we rarely experience events worthy of embodiment in a narrative. For children, this problem is even more pronounced. Younger writers often don't have the life experiences necessary to write about a broad range of topics. This is probably the biggest challenge in teaching narrative writing because it is the one instructors can do the least about. Any teacher of writing has read his or her fill of narratives about surprise birthday parties, trips to theme parks, and the arrival of new puppies. Furthermore, students have often used these same narratives before, in earlier grades, and attempt to recycle them because they honestly can't think of anything else.
Solution. Gravitate toward fiction. Fiction writing opens up an entire new universe of topics for developing writers. Instead of writing about a real first trip to the dentist, students can describe an imaginary first trip to Mars. Since both non-fiction and fictional narratives should contain most of the same writing elements, transitioning students from one into the other should be relatively painless.

Challenge #2: Lack of a conflict. Adolescence may be a time of conflict in the lives of young teens, but you'd have a hard time discerning it from their narratives. Many young writers omit conflict from their narratives altogether. Tales of fun (or sad) days abound, but these are really anecdotes rather than full-fledged narratives.
Solution. Provide explicit instruction. Teaching students about the importance of conflict early

in the writing process is crucial. Placing students in writing workstations designed to teach them about conflict is a good place to start. (See the mini-lesson and workstation, "Writing the Body: Conflict" on pages 112-113.) In addition, having students identify the conflicts in the narratives they are reading highlights the role of conflicts in narratives and acts as a springboard when developing narrative ideas.

Challenge #3: Lack of narrative significance. Student writing will frequently feature events that are of significance to the writer but not to the audience. It can be difficult for young writers to comprehend that their best day may be of little interest to a reader, unless the reader can take away a lesson or a universal truth from the narrative.

Solution. Teach significance first. Doing this at the very beginning of the writing process prevents this problem from occurring in the first place. Telling a young writer that his or her narrative lacks significance once writing is underway is already too late. Use the mini-lesson and workstation, "Writing the Body: Narrative Significance," in **Chapter 10** before students start writing. If students can't state the significance of their narrative in a single sentence, send them back to consider it again before allowing them to write. Their narratives will improve dramatically.

CHOOSING LESSONS TO TEACH

The task and rubric at the end of this chapter may be reproduced and given to students as is, or you may modify them to meet the needs of your class. The task is simple enough to be used as a baseline writing assignment at the beginning of the year to assist you in determining proper student placement in workstations. To ensure success, you should teach the following mini-lessons (at a minimum) to cover the skills asked for in the task.

- Finding Topics: Narratives . . . 52
- Writing the Body: Narrative Significance . . . 114
- Writing the Body: CPR—Character, Problem, Resolution . . . 110
- Beginning Techniques: Setting . . . 60
- Descriptive Writing: Sensory Details . . . 134
- Writing Dialogue: Credible Conversations . . . 102
- Ending Techniques: Lessons Learned . . . 80
- Point of View: First-person Point of View . . . 96

Please note that these mini-lessons and workstations are the minimum necessary to teach what is asked of students on the task. Additional mini-lessons and workstation tasks can be taught as needed. Refer to page 164 in the **Teaching Resources** section for a full list of skill lessons that apply to narrative writing.

BUILDING STYLE INTO NARRATIVES

Narratives can benefit from almost any of the composing Target Skill lessons, so building style into student writing is as easy as teaching one of those lessons. Choose the ones you think your students need to learn, and let them at it! These lessons in particular will challenge students to think of their writing in new ways.

Teach *in medias res.* Students almost always tell narratives in strict chronological order. Teaching them to start *in medias res* ("in the middle of things") not only teaches them a new beginning technique, it gets them thinking about narrative structure as a whole.

Teach point of view. Because their narratives are often either true or based on true life experiences, students tend to write in the first person. Teaching them omniscient and limited-omniscient point of view can get them writing from a new angle and expand their writing repertoire.

Teach suspense. Any teacher with a few years under his or her belt has read countless narratives that begin something like this: *I'm going to tell you about the time I saved my little brother from getting bitten by a dog.* These narratives drain all suspense from student writing at the very outset. Giving explicit instruction in suspense can help make narratives much more exciting.

Teach personification. This is an oft neglected literary device that can add a unique touch to narratives. Adding personification to descriptions of places or objects lends sparkle to narrative writing.

WRITING NARRATIVES ACROSS THE CURRICULUM

Narratives are generally considered the province of language arts teachers, but they can easily be incorporated into other subject areas. Here are some tasks to help you implement narrative writing across the curriculum.

Social studies. Students can write a memoir about a famous historical event from the point of view of a participant in that event. A concurrent reading of historical fiction from the same time period makes for an engaging unit, culminating in student readings of their own fictionalized pieces.

Science. Rather than just report on a famous scientist, why not have students take on the persona of a famous scientist? From there, have students relate, in narrative form, the life of the scientist, ending with his or her greatest discovery or invention.

Math. Students can write a fictional narrative showing how a character solves a real-life problem by using math skills. An easy way to do this is to instruct students to write narratives in which the conflict between the characters revolves around money, land, or any other dispute that can be resolved mathematically.

USING THE TASK AND RUBRIC FOR WRITING A NARRATIVE

The following pages contain a reproducible task and rubric. Give a copy of the task to each student before drafting begins. This sets the expectations for the writing piece. The rubric should be used to score student writing after drafting is completed and will let both you and your students know what areas need additional revision.

Task for a Narrative—"A Significant Loss"

Write about a time you lost something that was of great value to you. It can be something physical, such as a personal possession, an important person in your life, or a special pet. It can also be something intangible, such as trust, friendship, loyalty, or love. Write about why this loss was significant to you. Your job is to make the reader feel your loss.

In your narrative, be sure to:

☐ Start by describing where and when the action begins.

☐ Write from your own point of view (first person).

☐ Use sensory details to describe who or what you lost.

☐ Tell how you suffered this loss.

☐ Discuss events in a logical order and leave out unnecessary details.

☐ Include important dialogue.

☐ Clearly show the significance of your loss.

☐ Conclude by discussing what you learned from this event.

Remember to check your paper for correct spelling, grammar, punctuation, and paragraphing.

Rubric for a Narrative—"A Significant Loss"

IN YOUR NARRATIVE, DID YOU:

4: OUTSTANDING	3: GOOD	2: NEEDS IMPROVEMENT	1: NOT DONE
Begin by clearly establishing the time and place?			
Establishes the time and place effectively through description.	Establishes the time and place through description.	Attempts to establish the time and place, but description is lacking or needs development.	No attempt to establish the time and place or no attempt to describe it.
Establish its significance?			
Significance is clearly shown. The lesson learned through your loss is important and well developed.	Significance of your narrative is shown. The lesson learned through your loss is an interesting one.	Attempts to establish significance of the loss, but it is not clearly shown or needs more development.	Significance of the loss is unclear or absent.
Effectively use CPR to develop a clear, logical plot?			
Effectively uses CPR. The plot is logically constructed and clear to the reader.	Good use of CPR. The plot is generally clear and logical.	Some elements of CPR are missing or unclear. Plot needs development.	Inadequate use of CPR. Plot is difficult to follow or seems out of sequence.
Engage the reader through effective use of dialogue and sensory detail?			
Engages the reader through highly effective use of dialogue and sensory detail.	Engages the reader through use of dialogue and sensory detail.	Use of dialogue and/or sensory detail needs work.	Use of dialogue and/or sensory detail is missing.
Establish a first-person point of view that is consistently used throughout the piece?			
Establishes a consistent first-person point of view that helps tell the narrative effectively.	Establishes a mostly consistent first-person point of view that helps tell the narrative.	Point of view is present but sometimes switches between first person, omniscient, and limited omniscient.	Point of view is unclear or keeps switching between first person, omniscient, and limited omniscient.
Exclude unnecessary details?			
Contains no unnecessary details.	Contains only a few unnecessary details that do not interfere with the narrative.	Contains more than a few unnecessary details that may interfere with reader understanding.	Contains many unnecessary details that confuse the reader about the focus of the narrative.

COMMENTS:

Writing a Literary Response

ELEMENTS OF A LITERARY RESPONSE

The most basic definition of a literary response is a writing assignment resulting from reading. It can take numerous forms. There are traditional book reports, book reviews, letters to the author, postcards to characters, and so forth. Whatever the assignment, it is crucial that students learn to apply critical thinking to their responses. Good literary response tasks will ask student writers to make a judgment and back it up with specific references to the text.

The maturation process of your student authors depends largely on the extent to which they achieve independence of thought. Assigning a "one-size-fits-all" topic that most students can easily produce serves little educational purpose. For student authors to begin writing meaningful responses, they should take ownership of their piece through topic selection. Teachers can facilitate this by crafting tasks that encourage, rather than limit, student choice of topic.

THE CHALLENGES OF LITERARY-RESPONSE WRITING

Challenge #1: Being too explicit in writing tasks. Having been guilty of it many times myself, I know how tempting it is to write detailed tasks for students. Many is the time I have dictated not only the topic, but the length, number of paragraphs, types of support needed, and whatever else I could think of in an attempt to "assist" students in writing a cogent piece. Not surprisingly, I usually got back what I asked for—cookie-cutter responses bereft of any meaningful student thought. Solution. Make your tasks more general. To begin with, leave off any mention of word count, paragraph length, or number of examples needed when writing your task. Instead, focus on getting your students to choose meaty topics that will lend themselves to deep exploration.

Challenge #2: Finding meaningful topics. Just as it is easy to be too explicit when writing tasks, it is equally easy to simply assign the topic. After all, as knowledgeable readers, we know the topics that best fit the reading. However, the fact that students don't always know what good topics are is precisely the reason we ought to let them figure it out for themselves. Solution. Let students explore. Give students both the time and the guidance they need to generate topics. Analyzing their reading for topics will lead to deeper understanding of the text and, ultimately, to more enthusiastic responses. Teach students the mini-lesson, "Finding Topics:

Literary Responses," and assign workstations based upon the outcome. As students progress through the workstations and begin compiling ideas, guide them into choosing those topics that will best lend themselves to development into a full response.

Challenge #3: Lack of supporting details. Finding an exciting topic is of little use if students find themselves unable to support their ideas with valid examples from the text. Great topics sometimes fizzle out because students lack the skill to find support for them. Discovering supporting details reinforces the validity of student topics and moves the writing process forward.

Solution. Provide explicit instruction on finding supporting details. Finding supporting details is a skill that can be learned. Teach the mini-lesson, "Creating Paragraphs: Supporting Details," and assign workstation tasks as needed.

CHOOSING LESSONS TO TEACH

The task and rubric at the end of this chapter may be reproduced and given to students as is, or you may modify them to meet the needs of your class. The task is simple enough to be used as a baseline writing assignment at the beginning of the year to assist you in determining proper student placement in workstations. To ensure success, you should teach the following mini-lessons (at a minimum) to cover the skills asked for in the task:

- Finding Topics: Literary Responses . . . 54
- Finding Topics: Narrowing Your Focus . . . 56
- Creating Paragraphs: Topic Sentences . . . 68
- Creating Paragraphs: Supporting Details . . . 70
- Beginning Techniques: Lead Types—Questions, Descriptions, and Bold Statements . . . 66
- Writing the Body: Compare/contrast . . . 122
- Creating Paragraphs: Time Transitions . . . 72
- Ending Techniques: Ending Types—Restate the Main Idea, Make a Recommendation, and Make a Prediction . . . 82

Please note that these mini-lessons and workstations are the minimum necessary to teach what is asked of students on the task. Additional mini-lessons and workstation tasks can be taught as needed. Refer to page 165 in the **Teaching Resources** section for a full list of skill lessons that apply to writing literary responses.

BUILDING STYLE INTO LITERARY RESPONSES

Your approach to teaching students to add their own style to literary responses depends largely on what type of response you ask them to write. If you ask for a narrative written in the same style or genre as the reading, almost any composing Target Skill will help. If you ask for students to discuss some aspect of their reading, details and support will necessarily make up the body, and you'll need to rely on creative leads and endings to help students inject their own style into the essay.

Like narratives, literary responses are often thought to be the exclusive domain of language arts teachers. However, since all subjects involve reading, they all present opportunities to write literary responses. Here are some tasks to help you implement literary response writing across the curriculum.

Social studies. Students can read historical fiction related to the time period being studied. Responses can include explaining how faithful the characters are to the real people of the era, rewriting part of the book in a present-day setting, or writing letters to characters explaining how their actions have altered history.

Science. Students can read a biography of a scientist and respond by writing a resume for that person or explaining which traits of that person would make an interesting fictional character.

Art. Students can respond to their reading by drawing a picture of a character based upon a description in their book. They can surround the portrait with drawings of the setting, a tableau of the most important scene, and a picture that expresses the mood of the book.

USING THE TASK AND RUBRIC FOR WRITING A LITERARY RESPONSE

The following pages contain a reproducible task and rubric. Give a copy of the task to each student before drafting begins. This sets the expectations for the writing piece. The rubric should be used to score student writing after drafting is completed and will let both you and your students know what areas need additional revision.

Task for a Literary Response—"Character Virtues"

Fictional characters often display many virtues despite the challenges they face in life. Some of the virtues that the characters may exhibit include responsibility, courage, compassion, loyalty, honesty, friendship, hard work, self-discipline, and others.

In a well-written literary response, choose three virtues displayed by one of the characters in your book, and discuss the ways in which those virtues help the character overcome the obstacles in his or her life by using support/examples/quotes from the text. In addition, you must be able to make a connection between one of the character's virtues and your own life.

In your response, be sure to:

☐ Interest the reader with a strong introduction and your own ideas about the virtues your character possesses.

☐ Clearly express your own thoughts and feelings about the character and his or her actions.

☐ Support your ideas by referring to the text and giving specific examples.

☐ Demonstrate that you clearly understood the story.

☐ End your response with a strong conclusion.

Remember to check your paper for correct spelling, grammar, punctuation, and paragraphing.

Rubric for a Literary Response—"Character Virtues"

IN YOUR LITERARY RESPONSE, DID YOU:

4: OUTSTANDING	3: GOOD	2: NEEDS IMPROVEMENT	1: NOT DONE
Engage the reader with an interesting introduction that states your own ideas about the character?			
Introduction is strong and reveals a clear, original opinion about the virtues the character possesses.	Good introduction with a clear opinion about the virtues the character possesses.	Attempts to make a strong introduction but needs a stronger opinion or more engaging introduction.	Introduction is weak and/or doesn't include an opinion to engage the reader.
Express an opinion and support it with evidence from the text?			
Opinions are strong, insightful, and supported by excellent examples from the text.	Opinions are evident and supported with good examples from the text.	Opinions need revision and/or use limited examples/evidence from text.	Opinions are not apparent and/or not supported by examples/evidence from text.
Demonstrate an understanding of the text?			
Shows great insight into the story.	Shows a clear understanding of the text.	Shows limited understanding of text.	Does not show understanding of the text.
End with a strong conclusion?			
Strong conclusion that is concise, wraps up the essay, and revisits the main idea.	Strong conclusion summarizes the main points.	Attempts to revisit the main idea and wrap up the essay but needs improvement.	The conclusion doesn't summarize the main idea of the essay.
Use proper grammar, spelling and usage?			
Extremely well written with little or no grammar, spelling and usage mistakes.	Well written with few major errors.	Several mistakes, some of which may interfere with reader understanding.	Essay has many mistakes that hinder reader understanding.

COMMENTS:

9

Organizational Techniques: Target Skill Lessons and Workstation Tasks

Finding Topics

REPORTS

Reports are designed to give information to the reading audience. They are non-fiction. A report may be about a person (a biography), a place, or a subject of interest. A good way to start exploring topics is to explore what you already know.

WATCH how it's done. Here's a subject and some possible topics that might be suitable for a report.

SUBJECT: Solar System

Possible Topics: Mercury, Venus, Earth, Mars, Saturn, Jupiter, Uranus, Neptune, Pluto, orbits, moons, the sun, comets, asteroids, life on planets, space exploration

---

HELP with this subject. Using the subject "Earth," help brainstorm possible topics below for a report about the Earth:

Possible Topics:

APPLY this skill in your writing notebook. For each subject below, brainstorm a few possible report topics.

---

1. government
2. wars
3. inventions
4. marine animals
5. weather

MASTER this skill in your workstation.

Finding Topics

REPORTS

Reports are designed to give information to the reading audience. They are non-fiction. A report may be about a person (a biography), a place, or a subject of interest. A good way to start exploring topics is to explore what you already know.

Here's a subject and some possible topics that might be suitable for a report:

SUBJECT: Solar System

Possible Topics: Mercury, Venus, Earth, Mars, Saturn, Jupiter, Uranus, Neptune, Pluto, orbits, moons, the sun, comets, asteroids, life on planets, space exploration

TASK A	Your task is to brainstorm as many possible topics as you can. Divide your paper into four columns, and label them *people*, *places*, *things*, and *events*. Challenge yourself to fill as much of each column as you can.
TASK B	Choose two or three topics you think might make an interesting report. For each possible topic, write down what you already know about the topic and what you might have to find out.
TASK C	Once you have narrowed down your topics to one or two possibilities that have been approved by your teacher, start writing down what makes the topic(s) interesting to you. (If you can't think of anything, you probably need a different topic!) Then, think of what you believe your audience will find interesting about your topic. Rank those items from *most interesting* to *least interesting*.
TASK D	Select the topic of your report. Begin some preliminary drafting of your report in your notebook.

Finding Topics

PERSUASIVE ESSAYS

The purpose of a persuasive essay is to offer facts and opinions that will change the reader's mind about a topic. Interesting topics are those that have two strong sides to them. Your job as the writer is to choose one side and present it in such a way that your reader will be convinced. As you explore topics, make sure you understand both sides—both the *for* and the *against*.

WATCH how it's done.

TOPIC: Raising taxes

FOR: The money will help build new schools.

AGAINST: Taxes are already too high, and the old schools are fine.

HELP with these topics.

TOPIC: The need for more homework

FOR: Students might achieve higher scores on tests.

AGAINST:

TOPIC: Students creating the school lunch menus

FOR:

AGAINST: Students might not choose nutritious meals.

APPLY this skill in your writing notebook. Write a possible *for* and *against* for each of these topics:

1. More computers in the classroom
2. Building a new stadium in our town
3. Shortening the school year
4. Putting more police on the streets
5. Raising the voting age

MASTER this skill in your workstation.

Finding Topics

PERSUASIVE ESSAYS

The purpose of a persuasive essay is to offer facts and opinions that will change the reader's mind about a topic. Interesting topics are those that have two strong sides to them. Your job as the writer is to choose one side and present it in such a way that your reader will be convinced. As you explore topics, make sure you understand both sides—both the *for* and the *against*.

TASK A   Brainstorm as many topics as you can. Then create a chart like the one below. Decide whether each topic is local, national, or international by writing it in the appropriate column.

LOCAL	NATIONAL	INTERNATIONAL

TASK B   Choose some of the topics you thought of in Task A, or brainstorm some possible topics now. Choose five topics you think you might want to write about. For each one, write the topic, a possible *for* argument, and a possible *against* argument.

TASK C   Narrow your topics down to the two or three you think would be interesting for you to discuss in your persuasive essay. For each one, begin exploring what you already know about the topic and what you might have to do research on.

TASK D   Select the topic of your persuasive essay. Begin some preliminary drafting of your essay in your notebook.

Finding Topics

Mini-lesson

HOW-TO (PROCEDURAL) ESSAYS

How-to essays tell the reader exactly that: how to do something step by step. Topics range from easy to difficult. You can write about how to tie shoelaces, how to solve math problems, or how to build bridges. The key to finding a good topic is choosing an area you are expert in or that you can effectively research.

WATCH   how it's done. Notice that if you leave out a single step, the reader may fail.

TOPIC: How to use your television's new remote control

1. Place two fresh AA batteries in your remote. Follow the diagram on the back of the remote to see which way to place the batteries.
2. Point your remote at the TV.
3. Make sure nothing blocks the path from the remote to the TV.
4. Press the green "ON" button on your remote.
5. Use the numeric keypad to select the channel you want to watch.
6. Enjoy!

HELP   with this how-to topic. List the steps needed to complete this task.

TOPIC: How to study for a test

1. Find a quiet place to work.

2.

3.

4.

5.

APPLY   this skill in your writing notebook. List the steps for these how-to topics.

---

1. How to make lemonade
2. How to add two-digit numbers

MASTER   this skill in your workstation.

Finding Topics

Workstation

HOW-TO (PROCEDURAL) ESSAYS

How-to essays tell the reader exactly that: how to do something step by step. Topics range from easy to difficult. You can write about how to tie shoelaces, how to solve math problems, or how to build bridges. The key to finding a good topic is choosing an area you are expert in or that you can effectively research.

TOPIC: How to use your television's new remote control

1. Place two fresh AA batteries in your remote. Follow the diagram on the back of the remote to see which way to place the batteries.
2. Point your remote at the TV.
3. Make sure nothing blocks the path from the remote to the TV.
4. Press the green "ON" button on your remote.
5. Use the numeric keypad to select the channel you want to watch.
6. Enjoy!

TASK A
Explore the things that you are expert at. Brainstorm a list of topics that you think you know well enough to explain to someone who is a complete beginner. Then, for each topic, explain what qualifies you as an expert. For example:

TOPIC	WHAT MAKES ME AN EXPERT
How to bunt a baseball	I played Little League for three years.
How to multiply fractions	I got 100 on my last fractions test.

TASK B
Choose two or three topics you think might make an interesting how-to essay. For each possible topic, write down what you already know about the topic and what you might have to find out.

TASK C
Choose two or three topics you think might make an interesting how-to essay. List the steps for each topic. Decide which steps might need a definition or a graphic to help the reader understand the step. Draw some basic graphics, or look up some definitions and add them to the steps.

TASK D
Select the topic of your how-to essay. Begin some preliminary drafting of your essay in your notebook.

Finding Topics

Mini-lesson

The purpose of a narrative is to tell about an event. It may be a true life event (a personal narrative), or it may be fictional. A great way to find topics for your own narratives is to explore the events that have happened to you or people you know and to recall fictional stories that you've read in books or seen in the movies or on TV.

WATCH how it's done. Here's a list of personal experiences and fictional stories that could be used to generate topics:

PERSONAL EXPERIENCES	FICTIONAL STORIES
My embarrassing school play audition	A fight with a bully
My most memorable birthday	The day the aliens landed
My bad luck streak	Winning the Olympic Decathlon
My first trip to the principal	Twins switched at birth
My visit to the animal shelter	Winning a million dollars

HELP with this class list of topics. Add some personal and fictional stories to each column.

PERSONAL EXPERIENCES	FICTIONAL STORIES

APPLY this skill in your writing notebook. Create your own chart, and brainstorm some personal experiences as well as some fictional stories you've read or seen.

MASTER this skill in your workstation.

Finding Topics

Workstation

NARRATIVES

The purpose of a narrative is to tell about an event. It may be a true life event (a personal narrative), or it may be fictional. A great way to find topics for your own narratives is to explore the events that have happened to you or people you know and to recall fictional stories that you've read in books or seen in the movies or on TV.

TASK A   Use your classroom library to help you generate topics. Examine books, short stories, and even poems, and take notes of what they are about. Once you have a fairly large list, examine the topics, and place a check next to the ones you think might make an interesting topic for you to adapt for your own narrative.

TASK B   Use the list of personal experience topics you created during the mini-lesson. Place a check next to the ones you think would make the best stories, and then write a sentence explaining why you chose each one. When you are done, exchange lists with a partner and see if he or she agrees on which ones are best.

TASK C   Choose two or three of the topics you think will make a great narrative. Write a plot summary for each topic. Each summary should only be about a paragraph long and briefly tell the events that will take place in each narrative. When you are done, decide which summary will make the best narrative. Write a few sentences explaining your decision.

TASK D   Select the topic of your narrative. Begin some preliminary drafting in your notebook.

Finding Topics   # Mini-lesson

LITERARY RESPONSES

A literary response is designed to discuss something you have read. These responses can take many forms, such as a letter to the author, a book report, an essay, a rewrite of a story, and many more. The key to a good response is knowledge of the author or the stories you are responding to. Exploring what you know will help you develop a topic.

WATCH   how it's done.

WHAT I KNOW ABOUT VIRGINIA HAMILTON:

1. Books and stories: *Zeely*; *The People Could Fly*; *M.C. Higgins, the Great*; *Anthony Burns*; *Many Thousand Gone*
2. Themes: Freedom, slavery, courage, belonging
3. Characters: Zeely, Brother Rush, He Lion, Bruh Bear, Bruh Rabbit, Nehemiah
4. Genres: Historical fiction, non-fiction, folk tales
5. Other observations: Uses authentic language, strong characters, magical events

---

HELP   with this sentence, using an author we have recently read.

WHAT I KNOW ABOUT

1. Books and stories:

2. Themes:

3. Characters:

4. Genres:

5. Other observations:

APPLY   this skill in your writing notebook. Think of an author you have recently read, either from your independent reading or something we have read in class. Use the same format as above to record information about the author.

MASTER   this skill in your workstation.

Finding Topics

LITERARY RESPONSES

A literary response is designed to discuss something you have read. These responses can take many forms, such as a letter to the author, a book report, an essay, a rewrite of a story, and many more. The key to a good response is knowledge of the author or the stories you are responding to. Exploring what you know will help you develop a topic.

TASK A Make two columns on your page. Label one *Authors I Enjoy* and the other *Stories I Enjoy*. Brainstorm as many entries for each column as you can. When you are done, see if any patterns emerge. Do your favorite authors write the same types of stories? Are your favorite stories usually from the same genre? Are the types of characters in the stories you enjoy similar? Note any other patterns that occur to you. Write them all in your notebook.

TASK B Literary responses often call on you to make comparisons (showing what is similar) and contrasts (showing what is different). Making Venn diagrams can help you discover topics by showing you what does and doesn't compare. Choose two authors or two stories by the same author, and create a Venn diagram about them.

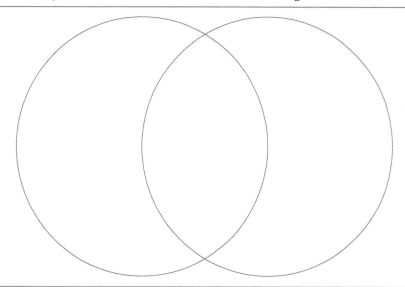

TASK C If you can find three similarities between stories, you have the makings of an excellent topic. Examine stories you have read. See if you can find three that have:

- The same or similar themes
- The same or similar characters
- The same or similar writing techniques
- The same or similar conflicts

TASK D Select the topic of your literary response. Begin some preliminary drafting of your response in your notebook.

Finding Topics

NARROWING YOUR FOCUS

Once you find an exciting topic to write about, you may want to simply jump into writing it. Not so fast! Some topics are just too big to discuss completely and need to be narrowed down. By focusing on a narrow area of your topic, you'll be able to cover it better and give the reader the information he or she needs.

WATCH how it's done

ORIGINAL TOPIC: Baseball

NARROWER TOPICS:

(How-to essay) How to throw a curveball

(Persuasive essay) Should players be tested for steroids?

(Report) The top three stadiums in the major leagues

(Narrative) The time I won the big game

HELP with this topic. Narrow the focus of the topic so that it will be appropriate for each genre:

TOPIC: Homework

(How-to essay)

(Persuasive essay)

(Report)

(Narrative)

APPLY this skill in your writing notebook. For each topic below, think of some narrower subtopics that would make a more focused writing piece.

---

1. Outer space
2. Presidents
3. Music

MASTER this skill in your workstation.

Finding Topics

NARROWING YOUR FOCUS

Once you find an exciting topic to write about, you may want to simply jump into writing it. Not so fast! Some topics are just too big to discuss completely and need to be narrowed down. By focusing on a narrow area of your topic, you'll be able to cover it better and give the reader the information he or she needs.

ORIGINAL TOPIC: Baseball

NARROWER TOPICS:

(How-to essay) How to throw a curveball

(Persuasive essay) Should players be tested for steroids?

(Report) The top three stadiums in the major leagues

(Narrative) The time I won the big game

TASK A
Practice narrowing some topics. Each of the topics below is too broad for an essay. Focus each topic by looking for narrow areas that you can explore completely. Think of as many narrow areas as you can for each topic. The first one has been done for you.

• Weather—storms, lightning, rain, how to protect yourself from a hurricane

• Sports

• Government

• Science

• My community

TASK B
Gather some non-fiction books on a variety of topics. Record the topic of each book in your writing notebook. Then, look at the table of contents and index to find out which subtopics are discussed, and record those as well. Place a check next to any subtopic that you think might make a narrow enough topic for a short report, how-to essay, or persuasive essay.

TASK C
Examine the topics you have explored for your own essay, and make a list of them in your writing notebook. Think about each one and whether the topic is really narrow enough for you to discuss completely. If it is, place a check next to it. If it is still too broad, work on narrowing it. Then check off that topic as well.

TASK D
Choose one of the narrow topics you have crafted, and begin drafting it. If you discover that the topic is still too broad, narrow it further before continuing your draft.

Beginning Techniques

DIALOGUE

There are many great ways to grab the reader's attention as you begin a writing piece. One of them is through the use of interesting dialogue. Engaging the reader through dialogue propels the reader into the minds of your characters from the opening lines of your narrative.

WATCH   how it's done

ORIGINAL OPENING:

One day I really remember is the time I convinced my mother to take us on the big roller coaster ride.

REVISED OPENING USING DIALOGUE:

"Mom, please let me go! All the other kids my age have done it!" I whined.

"Not on your life," she insisted. "If you think I'm letting you go on that death trap of a roller coaster, you're crazy."

Notice how the revised opening lets the reader know what each character feels.

HELP   with this opening.

ORIGINAL OPENING:

The first time I went to the dentist, I was scared silly. When he pulled out the drill, I knew I was in trouble.

REVISED OPENING:

APPLY   this skill in your writing notebook. Write an opening with dialogue in which two characters have opposite emotions about the same event. For example, you may write a dialogue between two runners in a race, the winner and the last-place finisher. Write dialogue that reflects the emotions each would feel.

MASTER this skill in your workstation.

Beginning Techniques

DIALOGUE

There are many great ways to grab the reader's attention as you begin a writing piece. One of them is through the use of interesting dialogue. Engaging the reader through dialogue propels the reader into the minds of your characters from the opening lines of your narrative.

ORIGINAL OPENING:

One day I really remember is the time I convinced my mother to take us on the big roller coaster ride.

REVISED OPENING USING DIALOGUE:

"Mom, please let me go! All the other kids my age have done it!" I whined.

"Not on your life," she insisted. "If you think I'm letting you go on that death trap of a roller coaster, you're crazy."

Notice how the revised opening lets the reader know what each character feels.

TASK A	Write a potential opening sentence using dialogue for each of these emotions: sadness, happiness, disgust, fear, and disappointment. For example, if the emotion is *sadness*, what might your character say to show that he or she is feeling sad?

TASK B	As in Task A, write a potential opening sentence using dialogue for each of these emotions: surprise, weariness, impatience, joy, and love. In addition, have another character respond in dialogue to the first character. For example, if the first character expresses fear in his or her words, how might the second character respond? Remember that the second character may respond with a different emotion—he or she may respond in surprise to the first character's fear.

TASK C	Write an opening using only dialogue between two or more characters. Clearly show the emotion of the main character as well as how other characters respond to him or her.

TASK D	Select a piece from your draft folder or your writing notebook that could benefit from an improved opening. Write the opening dialogue, and see whether it improves your piece.

Beginning Techniques

SETTING

An excellent way to engage your reader's interest is to create a mood by describing the setting of your narrative. Remember that setting describes the where and when of your narrative.

Engaging the reader through setting plunges the reader into the world of your characters. It also lets the reader know, from the very beginning of your narrative, what type of narrative to expect. A great setting helps create a great narrative!

WATCH   how it's done

ORIGINAL OPENING:

I had a really scary day during the blackout of 2004. Everything was dark, and I didn't know what was happening.

REVISED OPENING USING SETTING TO CREATE A MOOD:

I was alone in my bedroom listening to the rain pound against the window. The single bulb that hung from the center of the room cast just enough light for me to do my homework. I loved the quiet of my bedroom because it allowed me to concentrate on my assignments. I wrote my name and the date, June 24, 2004, at the top of a fresh sheet of white paper when the lights went dim and then went out. The room was draped in total darkness. I could see nothing, and all I could hear was the beat of the rain. Suddenly there was a flash of lightning that cast a brief but ghostly light on the room.

Notice how the revised opening lets the reader feel what the character feels.

HELP   with this opening.

ORIGINAL OPENING:

The happiest moment of my life was my fifth birthday party. Everyone I knew was there. There was music and food and decorations.

REVISED OPENING:

APPLY   this skill in your writing notebook. Write an opening paragraph about an important event in your life. Describe the setting so that the reader feels what you felt.

MASTER   this skill in your workstation.

Beginning Techniques

Workstation

SETTING

An excellent way to engage your reader's interest is to create a mood by describing the setting of your narrative. Remember that setting describes the where and when of your narrative.

Engaging the reader through setting plunges the reader into the world of your characters. It also lets the reader know, from the very beginning of your narrative, what type of narrative to expect. A great setting helps create a great narrative!

ORIGINAL OPENING:

I had a really scary day during the blackout of 2004. Everything was dark, and I didn't know what was happening.

REVISED OPENING USING SETTING TO CREATE A MOOD:

I was alone in my bedroom listening to the rain pound against the window. The single bulb that hung from the center of the room cast just enough light for me to do my homework. I loved the quiet of my bedroom because it allowed me to concentrate on my assignments. I wrote my name and the date, June 24, 2004, at the top of a fresh sheet of white paper when the lights went dim and then went out. The room was draped in total darkness. I could see nothing, and all I could hear was the beat of the rain. Suddenly there was a flash of lightning that cast a brief but ghostly light on the room.

Notice how the revised opening lets the reader feel what the character feels.

TASK A For each of the places listed below, make a list of words that might help the reader visualize the setting of that place.

---

1. A carnival
2. A sports stadium
3. A haunted house
4. A library

TASK B Create a table in your notebook like the one below. For each place, give an example of what you might see, hear, smell, touch, and taste in that place.

PLACE	SEE	HEAR	SMELL	TOUCH	TASTE
restaurant	waiter	music	coffee	napkin	cake
kitchen					
theater					
circus					

TASK C Write an opening that thoroughly describes a place. Choose a place that is familiar to you, and describe it by showing the reader what you see, hear, smell, touch, and taste.

TASK D Select a piece from your draft folder or your writing notebook that could benefit from an improved opening. Write a paragraph to thoroughly describe the setting of the narrative using sensory details.

Mini-lesson

IN MEDIAS RES

The term *in medias res* means "in the middle of things." Most stories start at the beginning. One way to make your narrative stand out is to begin it in the middle! By briefly previewing for your reader an exciting plot event, you create suspense. First, make sure you understand the events of your own narrative in time order. Then choose an exciting moment from somewhere in the middle that would be sure to intrigue your reader, and begin *in medias res*! (Remember, you're only teasing the reader with what's to come. Don't give too much of the narrative away.)

When you've completed such an opening, go back to the beginning of the narrative and tell it in normal time order. You reader will want to discover the events that led to such a dramatic moment.

WATCH   how it's done

OPENING USING *in medias res*:

The roller coaster clanked higher and higher toward the scariest peak of the ride. My palms were sweaty with anticipation. All I could see was the blue sky above me. I gripped the edges of my seat with all my might and silently prayed that this ordeal would be over soon. The ride groaned and sputtered and clanked some more as it reached the top. And then—silence. Stillness. No motion or sound at all. We were stuck inches from the top of the scariest ride ever created.

It all began that morning when my brother Joe challenged me to get on the Cardiac Coaster. I told him there was no way….

HELP   with this example. Pretend we're writing a narrative about a girl who lost her beloved dog. Write an opening that starts with the moment the dog breaks away from her.

OPENING USING *in medias res*:

APPLY   this skill in your writing notebook. Think of an exciting narrative that happened to you, and write an opening for it that begins *in medias res*.

MASTER   this skill in your workstation.

Beginning Techniques

Workstation

IN MEDIAS RES

The term *in medias res* means "in the middle of things." Most stories start at the beginning. One way to make your narrative stand out is to begin it in the middle! By briefly previewing for your reader an exciting plot event, you create suspense. First, make sure you understand the events of your own narrative in time order. Then choose an exciting moment from somewhere in the middle that would be sure to intrigue your reader, and begin *in medias res*! (Remember, you're only teasing the reader with what's to come. Don't give too much of the narrative away.)

When you've completed such an opening, go back to the beginning of the narrative and tell it in normal time order. You reader will want to discover the events that led to such a dramatic moment.

OPENING USING *in medias res*:

The roller coaster clanked higher and higher toward the scariest peak of the ride. My palms were sweaty with anticipation. All I could see was the blue sky above me. I gripped the edges of my seat with all my might and silently prayed that this ordeal would be over soon. The ride groaned and sputtered and clanked some more as it reached the top. And then—silence. Stillness. No motion or sound at all. We were stuck inches from the top of the scariest ride ever created.

It all began that morning when my brother Joe challenged me to get on the Cardiac Coaster. I told him there was no way....

TASK A Create a timeline in your notebook using the events below, and circle the events that you think are the most suspenseful. Put a star next to the event that you think would be the best choice for creating an *in medias res* opening. Then write the opening.

---

1. We planned a day at the park.	5. I realized I had no money.
2. We packed a lunch.	6. The waiter made a scene.
3. I forgot to bring the lunch.	7. The waiter threatened to call the police.
4. We went to restaurant instead.	8. The police unexpectedly loaned me money.

TASK B Create a timeline like the one in Task A for a narrative that actually happened to you. Identify the most suspenseful moments of the narrative by circling them on your timeline. Place a star next to the event that you think would be the best opening moment for a narrative beginning *in medias res*. Then write the opening.

TASK C Think of a dramatic event that actually happened to you. Choose the most suspenseful moment of that event to write an *in medias res* opening for a potential future narrative.

TASK D Select a piece from your draft folder or your notebook that could be improved with a new opening. Write an *in medias res* opening for the piece.

Beginning Techniques

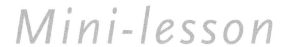

LEAD TYPES—INTERESTING FACTS, QUOTATIONS, AND ANECDOTES

A lead is the opening sentence or sentences of a non-fiction writing piece. Lead writing is critical for reports, persuasive essays, and how-to essays. A good lead will get the reader's attention immediately and make him want to read more. Your lead should also set the tone for the rest of the piece. For example, a lighthearted piece needs a lighthearted lead.

WATCH how it's done. Here are three types of leads.

INTERESTING FACT:

The cheetah can run up to seventy miles per hour and uses its long tail like a rudder to help it change direction at those incredible speeds.

QUOTATION:

"I never did anything worth doing by accident, nor did any of my inventions come by accident; they came by work," said Thomas Alva Edison, one of our country's greatest inventors.

ANECDOTE:

I learned how to build a go-cart the hard way when I hammered a nail through my thumb. There's an easier way for you to build one that won't end up with a trip to the emergency room.

HELP with creating some leads. Review your research on your topics, and come up with an example of an interesting fact, a quotation, and an anecdote.

INTERESTING FACT:

QUOTATION:

ANECDOTE:

APPLY this skill in your writing notebook. Review your research, and place an *I* next to interesting facts, a *Q* next to quotations, and an *A* next to anecdotes.

MASTER this skill in your workstation.

Workstation

LEAD TYPES—INTERESTING FACTS, QUOTATIONS, AND ANECDOTES

A lead is the opening sentence or sentences of a non-fiction writing piece. Lead writing is critical for reports, persuasive essays, and how-to essays. A good lead will get the reader's attention immediately and make him want to read more. Your lead should also set the tone for the rest of the piece. For example, a lighthearted piece needs a lighthearted lead.

INTERESTING FACT:

The cheetah can run up to seventy miles per hour and uses its long tail like a rudder to help it change direction at those incredible speeds.

QUOTATION:

"I never did anything worth doing by accident, nor did any of my inventions come by accident; they came by work," said Thomas Alva Edison, one of our country's greatest inventors.

ANECDOTE:

I learned how to build a go-cart the hard way when I hammered a nail through my thumb. There's an easier way for you to build one that won't end up with a trip to the emergency room.

TASK A INTERESTING FACTS: Review your research on your topic, and find all the facts that you think might make a great lead. Choose at least two, and write an opening paragraph for each that starts with that fact. When you are finished, choose which paragraph you think is the best and write a few sentences explaining why you think this paragraph will grab the reader's attention.

TASK B QUOTATIONS: Review your research on your topic, and find all the quotations that you think might make a great lead. Choose at least two, and write an opening paragraph for each that starts with that quotation. When you are finished, choose the one you think is best, and explain why the quotation will grab the reader's attention and how the quotation will help make your topic clear to the reader.

TASK C ANECDOTES: Review your research on your topic, and find all the anecdotes that you think might make a great lead. Choose at least two, and write an opening paragraph for each that starts with that anecdote. When you are finished, choose the one you think is best, and explain why the anecdote will grab the reader's attention and how it will help make your topic clear to the reader.

TASK D After you have tried out several lead types, choose the one you think will work best with your writing piece. Draft the lead and the rest of the opening paragraph. As you continue drafting the rest of your piece, make sure it fits with the tone of your lead.

Beginning Techniques

LEAD TYPES—QUESTIONS, DESCRIPTIONS, AND BOLD STATEMENTS

A lead is the opening sentence or sentences of a non-fiction writing piece. Lead writing is critical for reports, persuasive essays, and how-to essays. A good lead will get the reader's attention immediately and make him want to read more. Your lead should also set the tone for the rest of the piece. For example, a lighthearted piece needs a lighthearted lead.

WATCH how it's done. Here are three types of leads.

QUESTION:

What would it feel like to come face to face with the dreaded Komodo Dragon of Indonesia, a ten-foot-long lizard that can outrun any man?

DESCRIPTION:

Imagine standing on the steps of the Lincoln Memorial, surrounded by swarms of people on a hot August day in 1963. A look of hope crosses the faces of your fellow audience members as a solemn but determined man strides to the podium and announces, "I have a dream…"

BOLD STATEMENT:

If we don't tackle the problem of global warming today, we will see vast chunks of our country swallowed up by the melting arctic waters within our lifetimes.

HELP with creating some leads. Review your research on your topics, and come up with an example of a question, a description, and a bold statement.

QUESTION:

DESCRIPTION:

BOLD STATEMENT:

APPLY this skill in your writing notebook. Review your research, and place a question mark next to possible questions, a *D* next to descriptions, and a *B* next to information that would make a good bold statement.

MASTER this skill in your workstation.

LEAD TYPES—QUESTIONS, DESCRIPTIONS, AND BOLD STATEMENTS

A lead is the opening sentence or sentences of a non-fiction writing piece. Lead writing is critical for reports, persuasive essays, and how-to essays. A good lead will get the reader's attention immediately and make him want to read more. Your lead should also set the tone for the rest of the piece. For example, a lighthearted piece needs a lighthearted lead.

QUESTION:

What would it feel like to come face to face with the dreaded Komodo Dragon of Indonesia, a ten-foot-long lizard that can outrun any man?

DESCRIPTION:

Imagine standing on the steps of the Lincoln Memorial, surrounded by swarms of people on a hot August day in 1963. A look of hope crosses the faces of your fellow audience members as a solemn but determined man strides to the podium and announces, "I have a dream…"

BOLD STATEMENT:

If we don't tackle the problem of global warming today, we will see vast chunks of our country swallowed up by the melting arctic waters within our lifetimes.

TASK A QUESTIONS: Review your research on your topic, and find all the facts that you might be able to turn into an interesting question. Choose at least two, and write an opening paragraph for each that starts with that question. When you are finished, choose which paragraph you think is the best and write a few sentences explaining why you think this paragraph will grab the reader's attention.

TASK B DESCRIPTIONS: Review your research on your topic, and find all descriptions of the people and places in your topic that might make a great lead. Choose at least two, and write an opening paragraph for each that starts with that description. When you are finished, choose which paragraph you think is the best and write a few sentences explaining why you think this paragraph will grab the reader's attention.

TASK C BOLD STATEMENTS: Review your research on your topic, and find all the facts that you think might be turned into bold statements. Choose at least two, and write an opening paragraph for each that starts with that statement. When you are finished, choose which paragraph you think is the best and write a few sentences explaining why you think this paragraph will grab the reader's attention.

TASK D After you have tried out several lead types, choose the one you think will work best with your writing piece. Draft the lead and the rest of the opening paragraph. As you continue drafting the rest of your piece, make sure it fits with the tone of your lead.

Creating Paragraphs

TOPIC SENTENCES

Just as your writing piece has a topic, each paragraph in your piece must discuss a subtopic—a specific part of that topic. Therefore, each paragraph needs its own topic sentence to let the reader know what is being discussed. Topic sentences are often the first sentence in a paragraph, but you can experiment with placing them in the middle or at the end of your paragraphs as well. The key to great topic sentences is to understand your overall topic and then discover the subtopics you'll write about in each paragraph.

WATCH how it's done. Look at the paragraph topic sentences for the main topic.

MAIN TOPIC: How to bake a cake

Subtopic: Ingredients

Topic Sentence: First, you'll need to gather together all your ingredients.

Subtopic: Equipment

Topic Sentence: Next, make sure you have the proper size bowl and spoons.

Subtopic: Mixing

Topic Sentence: Now it's time to mix your ingredients into a rich batter.

HELP with this topic. Come up with some subtopics and topic sentences for the main topic of George Washington.

Subtopic: Birth

Topic Sentence: George Washington was born in 1732 in Virginia.

Subtopic:

Topic Sentence:

Subtopic:

Topic Sentence:

APPLY this skill in your writing notebook. List some possible subtopics and topic sentences for one the following topics: a how-to essay on adding two-digit numbers, a report on a foreign country, or a persuasive essay on the need for more firehouses in your community.

MASTER this skill in your workstation.

Creating Paragraphs

Workstation

TOPIC SENTENCES

Just as your writing piece has a topic, each paragraph in your piece must discuss a subtopic—a specific part of that topic. Therefore, each paragraph needs its own topic sentence to let the reader know what is being discussed. Topic sentences are often the first sentence in a paragraph, but you can experiment with placing them in the middle or at the end of your paragraphs as well. The key to great topic sentences is to understand your overall topic and then discover the subtopics you'll write about in each paragraph.

MAIN TOPIC: How to bake a cake

Subtopic: Ingredients
Topic Sentence: First, you'll need to gather together all your ingredients.

Subtopic: Equipment
Topic Sentence: Next, make sure you have the proper size bowl and spoons.

Subtopic: Mixing
Topic Sentence: Now it's time to mix your ingredients into a rich batter.

TASK A Choose at least two topics from the list below. Make a list of possible subtopics and topic sentences for each.

- How to pack for an enjoyable vacation
- Hot spots in our city
- The need for more physical education classes
- How to take notes in class effectively
- The worst problem in our neighborhood

TASK B Choose a few of the topics you have been exploring for your essay. For each topic, list possible subtopics and write a possible topic sentence for each subtopic. For example, if one of your topics is tropical fish, you'd write:

MAIN TOPIC: Keeping tropical fish
Subtopic: Feeding your fish
Topic Sentence: It is important to feed your fish the right type of food.

Continue with as many subtopics and topic sentences as you need.

TASK C When you have decided on a main topic for your essay, it's time to explore the subtopics you will need and to write topic sentences for those subtopics. First, make a list of subtopics. Then, write your topic sentences. After you are done, read your topic sentences to a partner and see if they make sense to him or her. Revise if needed.

TASK D Like narrative leads, topic sentences should be clear and interesting. Work on making your topic sentences better. After you've revised them, show the old and new sentences to a partner, and see if your partner agrees that they are improved. If not, work on revising them.

Creating Paragraphs

SUPPORTING DETAILS

Now that you know how to write a topic sentence, it's time to learn how to support it. Using specific details and facts to support your topic sentences influences readers to accept your idea and helps persuade them that your point of view is correct.

WATCH   how it's done.

TOPIC SENTENCE:

Shakespeare was a great writer.

Without supporting details and facts, your topic sentence seems like nothing more than an opinion. Watch how supporting your topic sentence makes it believable to your reader.

Shakespeare was a great writer. Although he died almost 400 years ago, his plays are still popular today. Virtually every high school and college in America teaches courses on Shakespeare. He wrote 60 plays in his lifetime, and even those who've never read his works recognize his more famous titles, such as *Hamlet*, *MacBeth*, *Romeo and Juliet*, and *A Midsummer Night's Dream*. He invented the Shakespearean sonnet and is considered one of the finest poets who ever lived.

HELP   with this topic sentence. Add supporting details that help support the idea.

TOPIC SENTENCE:

America is a wonderful country.

APPLY   this skill in your writing notebook. Write a paragraph that starts with this topic sentence: *The cell phone is a great invention.* Add several supporting details to your paragraph to support this topic sentence. Try adding an opinion, a fact, and a quote from a partner or someone in your group.

MASTER   this skill in your workstation.

Creating Paragraphs

Workstation

SUPPORTING DETAILS

Now that you know how to write a topic sentence, it's time to learn how to support it. Using specific details and facts to support your topic sentences influences readers to accept your idea and helps persuade them that your point of view is correct.

TASK A
REPORT: If you're writing an informational report, you must include facts and/or details to support your topic and subtopics. Refer back to the work you did on topic sentences in your writer's notebook. For each subtopic you created for your report, write at least three facts and/or details that you have found that help support your ideas. If there seem to be any subtopics that need additional support, write down what additional information you will need to find.

TASK B
PERSUASIVE ESSAY: To write an effective persuasive essay, you should try to include a mix of quotes, personal experiences, or expert opinions to help convince your reader. Refer back to the work you did on topic sentences in your writer's notebook. For each subtopic you created for your persuasive essay, list the quotes, personal experiences, or expert opinions you plan to use to support that subtopic. If you discover that you need additional quotes or expert opinions to help support a subtopic, make notes about who you might need to talk to or what you might need to research for additional support.

TASK C
HOW-TO ESSAY: For how-to or procedural pieces, you must follow up your subtopics with the steps needed to complete the procedure. Refer back to the work you did on topic sentences in your writer's notebook. For each subtopic you created for your how-to essay, list what is needed to complete that part of the process.

TASK D
LITERARY RESPONSE: For literary responses, you must find direct quotes from the text that support your ideas. For each subtopic in your literary response, find direct quotes that show your ideas to be correct.

Creating Paragraphs

TIME TRANSITIONS

Time transitions show your reader the sequence of events. By properly using transitions, your reader can easily follow the sequence. Use transitions in paragraphs when the time of the events changes within the paragraph. Use them at the beginning of a paragraph when the time has changed and the reader needs to be informed of the change. Some common transitional words and phrases are: *before, after, soon after, later, the next day, meanwhile, next, prior to, at the same time, tomorrow, next year, years later, now, once, in a short while, in the end, immediately,* etc.

WATCH how it's done.

ORIGINAL PARAGRAPH WITHOUT TRANSITIONS:

My brother was seven when he got his first bike. He learned to drive a car. He went to college.

REVISED PARAGRAPH USING TIME TRANSITIONS:

My brother was seven when he got his first bike. Ten years later, he learned to drive a car. Soon after, he went to college.

HELP with these sentences. Add time transitions to make the time of each event clearer.

ORIGINAL PARAGRAPH WITHOUT TRANSITIONS:

I adopted a dog. I taught him tricks. He got bigger. He got sick. I took him to the vet. He's well.

REVISED PARAGRAPH USING TIME TRANSITIONS:

APPLY this skill in your writing notebook. Write out the events that have happened to you so far today. Use time transitions to make it clear to the reader when each event happened.

MASTER this skill in your workstation.

Creating Paragraphs

Workstation

TIME TRANSITIONS

Time transitions show your reader the sequence of events. By properly using transitions, your reader can easily follow the sequence. Use transitions in paragraphs when the time of the events changes within the paragraph. Use them at the beginning of a paragraph when the time has changed and the reader needs to be informed of the change. Some common transitional words and phrases are: *before, after, soon after, later, the next day, meanwhile, next, prior to, at the same time, tomorrow, next year, years later, now, once, in a short while, in the end, immediately,* etc.

ORIGINAL PARAGRAPH WITHOUT TRANSITIONS:

My brother was seven when he got his first bike. He learned to drive a car. He went to college.

REVISED PARAGRAPH USING TIME TRANSITIONS:

My brother was seven when he got his first bike. Ten years later, he learned to drive a car. Soon after, he went to college.

TASK A REPORT: If your report is about the history of a place or a person, make sure that your transitions reflect the dates and times accurately. Create a timeline of events that will help you organize them. For events that are separated by at least a year, label them with the year they occurred. For events that are separated by less than a year, try using transitional words as labels.

TASK B PERSUASIVE ESSAY: The parts of a persuasive essay that usually contain time transitions are your discussions of the history of the issue and your recommendations for future actions. Review those sections of your essay yourself and then with a partner. Discuss whether additional time transitions are needed to make things clearer. If they are, make those revisions using transitional words.

TASK C HOW-TO ESSAY: For how-to or procedural pieces, time transitions are critical. Review your how-to essay yourself and then with a partner. Make sure that all necessary steps are present. Then check to make sure that you have clearly discussed how much time must elapse before taking the next step. Will your reader understand whether he or she needs to wait before performing the next step? If not, rewrite your time transitions to make your procedure clearer.

TASK D NARRATIVE: Create a timeline for your narrative. Make sure you, as the author, understand how much time elapses between events. You may do this by creating a timeline of the events of your plot. Then, make sure that your have used enough time transition words to make the time sequence clear to your reader. Have a partner or someone in your group check your transitions to make sure they make sense.

Ending Techniques

CIRCULAR CLOSING—A PLACE

A circular closing is one in which you return to an event, a phrase, or an idea that you used in your opening in order to bring your narrative to a conclusion. Readers find this type of closing very satisfying because it clearly signals the ending and gives your narrative a sense of closure. Returning to a place can create a satisfying closing by showing the reader what has changed since your first visit to that place.

WATCH how it's done.

OPENING:

My first trip to the dentist was a nightmare. The sound of the drill as I sat nervously in the waiting room made my teeth chatter. I picked up a magazine to pass the time, but I discovered that all I could do was turn the pages. I was too frightened by that awful sound to actually concentrate on the words.

Assuming that your narrative is about how your trip to the dentist turned out fine, you might write a closing such as this:

CIRCULAR CLOSING:

When I returned to the dentist's office a week later, the sound of the drill didn't bother me a bit. I waved a friendly hello to the receptionist and picked up a copy of *Glamour* magazine. I read an article on how straight teeth improve your whole look. I decided to ask the dentist whether I needed braces.

HELP with this opening by writing a circular conclusion:

OPENING:

The day was dark and dreary. Rain pattered against my bedroom window. I could hardly drag myself out of bed to get dressed. It was the day I was to meet my new classmates, and I dreaded the idea of making all new friends. I stood by the window, wondering if there was any chance of it raining hard enough to close school.

CIRCULAR CLOSING:

APPLY this skill in your writing notebook. Think of a time when your attitude about a place changed. Write just the opening and closing of that narrative. Describe how you felt about that place at first, and then write a closing showing how your attitude changed.

MASTER this skill in your workstation.

Ending Techniques

CIRCULAR CLOSING—A PLACE

A circular closing is one in which you return to an event, a phrase, or an idea that you used in your opening in order to bring your narrative to a conclusion. Readers find this type of closing very satisfying because it clearly signals the ending and gives your narrative a sense of closure. Returning to a place can create a satisfying closing by showing the reader what has changed since your first visit to that place.

OPENING:

My first trip to the dentist was a nightmare. The sound of the drill as I sat nervously in the waiting room made my teeth chatter. I picked up a magazine to pass the time, but I discovered that all I could do was turn the pages. I was too frightened by that awful sound to actually concentrate on the words.

Assuming that your narrative is about how your trip to the dentist turned out fine, you might write a closing such as this:

CIRCULAR CLOSING:

When I returned to the dentist's office a week later, the sound of the drill didn't bother me a bit. I waved a friendly hello to the receptionist and picked up a copy of *Glamour* magazine. I read an article on how straight teeth improve your whole look. I decided to ask the dentist whether I needed braces.

TASK A	Choose two of the places from the following list: a doctor's office, an amusement park, a friend's house, a toy store, a school, or a restaurant. Write about how someone's attitude about these places might change over time and what events might bring about such a change.
TASK B	Make a list of places that you've changed your attitude about over time. They may be places you hated at first but then came to like or places that you enjoyed but then came to dislike. For each place, write the reason for your change in attitude.
TASK C	Choose a place you wrote about in Task B. Write just the opening and closing paragraphs of the narrative. Make sure that in your closing, you return to the place you wrote about in your opening. The closing should reflect any changes in your attitude about that place.
TASK D	Select a piece from your draft folder or your notebook that might benefit from a circular closing. Rewrite your closing to re-visit the place where your narrative began. Write about any attitude changes toward that place. Make sure that the attitude change is justified by the events in the narrative.

Organizational Techniques: Target Skill Lessons and Workstation Tasks

Ending Techniques

CIRCULAR CLOSING—A PHRASE

A circular closing is one in which you return to an event, a phrase, or an idea that you used in your opening in order to bring your narrative to a conclusion. Readers find this type of closing very satisfying because it clearly signals the ending and gives your narrative a sense of closure. Returning to a phrase can emphasize a point you wanted to make, or it can show the reader a change in a character (does the character still believe in what he or she said at the beginning?).

WATCH   how it's done.

OPENING:

My grandfather was a wonderful man. He always had a smile and a kind word for everyone he met. When I was younger, I didn't always understand him, because he used to say weird stuff, like "It's always darkest before the dawn." I remember thinking, well, of course it is! It's nighttime before the dawn! It took a terrible event to make me understand that phrase, but I'll always remember my grandfather for having said it.

CIRCULAR CLOSING:

The days following my grandfather's death were the darkest of my life. But soon I began to think of all the wonderful things he taught me and how he would always remain in my heart. It was then that I finally understood how "it's always darkest before the dawn."

HELP   write a circular closing for this opening:

OPENING:

When I was ten, I begged my mom for a solid week to let me go camping with my friends. She told me, "Be careful what you wish for. You just might get it." I didn't realize how right she was until she finally gave in and let me go camping.

CIRCULAR CLOSING:

APPLY   this skill in your writing notebook. Write a circular closing for a narrative that contains the opening phrase *There are things worth fighting for.*

MASTER   this skill in your workstation.

Ending Techniques

CIRCULAR CLOSING—A PHRASE

A circular closing is one in which you return to an event, a phrase, or an idea that you used in your opening in order to bring your narrative to a conclusion. Readers find this type of closing very satisfying because it clearly signals the ending and gives your narrative a sense of closure. Returning to a phrase can emphasize a point you wanted to make, or it can show the reader a change in a character (does the character still believe in what he or she said at the beginning?).

OPENING:

My grandfather was a wonderful man. He always had a smile and a kind word for everyone he met. When I was younger, I didn't always understand him, because he used to say weird stuff, like "It's always darkest before the dawn." I remember thinking, well, of course it is! It's nighttime before the dawn! It took a terrible event to make me understand that phrase, but I'll always remember my grandfather for having said it.

CIRCULAR CLOSING:

The days following my grandfather's death were the darkest of my life. But soon I began to think of all the wonderful things he taught me and how he would always remain in my heart. It was then that I finally understood how "it's always darkest before the dawn."

TASK A — Choose two of the phrases below. Ponder how a narrative might end if it began with that phrase. For example, with the first phrase, the narrative will probably end up being the character's happiest day or saddest day.

1. I thought it would be the happiest day of my life.
2. She told me, "It's too good to be true."
3. I just couldn't forgive and forget.
4. I thought it was everything I ever wanted.
5. I didn't have a care in the world.

TASK B — Use one of the phrases above to write an opening and a circular closing for a potential narrative. Make sure you include the phrase in both paragraphs.

TASK C — Think of a phrase that you or someone you know uses all the time. Think about how you might turn that phrase into a narrative. Write the opening and a circular closing for the narrative, and consider writing the entire narrative if time permits.

TASK D — Select a piece from your draft folder or your notebook that could be improved by using a circular closing. Look particularly for any pieces that open with interesting phrases or dialogue.

Ending Techniques

CIRCULAR CLOSING—AN IDEA

A circular closing is one in which you return to an event, a phrase, or an idea that you used in your opening in order to bring your narrative to a conclusion. Readers find this type of closing very satisfying because it clearly signals the ending and gives your narrative a sense of closure. Returning to an idea you explored at the beginning of your narrative helps to emphasize the idea and signals the reader that you have finished exploring it.

WATCH how it's done.

OPENING STATING AN IDEA:

When I first met my best friend Sammy, I didn't really notice anything special about him. I soon found out, however, that he was the best friend a person could ever have.

CLOSING RETURNING TO AN IDEA:

So even though Sammy and I seemed like a mismatched pair of socks, we ended up as the best of friends. I've never had a better friend, and I doubt I ever will. He's the best.

HELP with this opening. Write a closing that returns to the idea presented in the opening:

OPENING STATING AN IDEA:

It started out as the worst day of my life. Everything was going wrong. All I wanted to do was go back to bed and pull the covers up over my head. But if I had done that, I would have missed what turned out to be one of the best days of my life.

CLOSING RETURNING TO AN IDEA:

APPLY this skill in your writing notebook. Write an opening and a closing for a possible future narrative. In the opening, state the idea of your narrative. In the closing, restate the idea to bring closure to the narrative.

MASTER this skill in your workstation.

Ending Techniques

CIRCULAR CLOSING—AN IDEA

A circular closing is one in which you return to an event, a phrase, or an idea that you used in your opening in order to bring your narrative to a conclusion. Readers find this type of closing very satisfying because it clearly signals the ending and gives your narrative a sense of closure. Returning to an idea you explored at the beginning of your narrative helps to emphasize the idea and signals the reader that you have finished exploring it.

OPENING STATING AN IDEA:

When I first met my best friend Sammy, I didn't really notice anything special about him. I soon found out, however, that he was the best friend a person could ever have.

CLOSING RETURNING TO AN IDEA:

So even though Sammy and I seemed like a mismatched pair of socks, we ended up as the best of friends. I've never had a better friend, and I doubt I ever will. He's the best.

TASK A   Start generating a list of ideas you might want to write about. Keep the ideas simple. Your task is to generate as many ideas as you can.

TASK B   Choose an idea you generated in Task A, or think of another idea you might want to write about. Make a list of plot events that might happen in that narrative, beginning and ending with your idea. For example, your list should look something like this:

1. I woke up thinking it would be a horrible day.
2. I stubbed my toe.
3. I was late for school.
4. I hit the winning home run for my team.
5. My horrible day turned into a great day.

Your list should be more detailed than the example above. Include as many plot events as you can. Each event should be related to the narrative idea.

TASK C   Try your hand at writing a narrative with a circular ending that restates an idea. You may use the list you created in Task B, or you may start from scratch with a new idea. Try to write your opening and closing paragraphs first, and fill in the details later. You may wish to complete this narrative for inclusion in your draft folder.

TASK D   Select a piece from your draft folder or your notebook that could be improved by using a circular ending. Look especially for pieces that begin with or state an idea in the opening paragraph.

Ending Techniques

LESSONS LEARNED

An excellent way to bring closure to your narrative is to discuss the lesson you (or your characters) learned from the events that took place in the narrative. Fables, for example, come right out and tell you the moral of the tale. While you may not want to be that obvious about it, ending with the lesson learned can help give meaning to the narrative and point out its significance.

WATCH how it's done.

ORIGINAL ENDING:

So that's the narrative of the time my best friend lied to me. I hope you enjoyed it! Bye!

REVISED ENDING WITH A LESSON LEARNED:

Even though I was hurt by my best friend's lie, I learned that trust must be earned to be of value. I trusted my friend without question, and I got hurt for my trouble. Next time, I'll know better.

HELP with this ending. Revise it so that it shows a lesson.

ORIGINAL ENDING:

I got in so much trouble! What a horrible time I had! Well, that's all!

REVISED ENDING WITH A LESSON LEARNED:

APPLY this skill in your writing notebook. Write a possible ending for this lesson: *Families should always stick together.*

MASTER this skill in your workstation.

Ending Techniques

LESSONS LEARNED

An excellent way to bring closure to your narrative is to discuss the lesson you (or your characters) learned from the events that took place in the narrative. Fables, for example, come right out and tell you the moral of the tale. While you may not want to be that obvious about it, ending with the lesson learned can help give meaning to the narrative and point out its significance.

ORIGINAL ENDING:

So that's the narrative of the time my best friend lied to me. I hope you enjoyed it! Bye!

REVISED ENDING WITH A LESSON LEARNED:

Even though I was hurt by my best friend's lie, I learned that trust must be earned to be of value. I trusted my friend without question, and I got hurt for my trouble. Next time, I'll know better.

TASK A   Choose one of the lessons below, and write a possible ending for it. You don't need to write the narrative—just make sure you have an ending that discusses the lesson!

1. Family is important.
2. You should try to be patient with others.
3. Kindness is its own reward.
4. Good things come to those who wait.
5. A true friend always stands by you.

TASK B   Make a list of lessons you may recall from books, stories, TV shows, movies, or your own experiences. Choose one of the lessons, and write a summary of the narrative and a possible ending for the narrative that discusses the lesson learned.

TASK C   Write a narrative about a lesson you learned, and end it by discussing that lesson.

TASK D   Select a piece from your draft folder or your notebook that teaches a lesson, and write a new ending for it. Make sure your ending discusses the lesson you or your character learned and that it brings closure to your narrative. If you like the new ending, rewrite your piece!

Ending Techniques

ENDING TYPES—RESTATE THE MAIN IDEA, MAKE A RECOMMEDATION, AND MAKE A PREDICTION

Writing an effective ending is critical for reports, persuasive essays, how-to essays, and literary responses. A good ending will focus the reader's attention by summarizing the discussion or by giving the reader something to think about. Try the three ending techniques described below.

WATCH how it's done. If your essay topic deals with the need for a new stoplight, you might end in these three different ways:

RESTATE THE MAIN IDEA:

So, as you can see, it is our duty to put a stoplight up at the corner of 14th and Main. Only by doing so can we protect the schoolchildren who must cross that street every day.

MAKE A RECOMMENDATION:

To ensure that we get the stoplight we need at 14th and Main, I recommend that every parent and child who crosses that street write a letter to the mayor demanding immediate action.

MAKE A PREDICTION:

If a stoplight isn't installed on 14th and Main soon, it won't be long before someone is seriously injured or possibly killed. Taking action now will prevent such a tragedy.

HELP with this example. Write each ending type for this topic: *My town is a wonderful city to visit.*

Restate the main idea:

Make a recommendation:

Make a prediction:

APPLY this skill in your writing notebook. Write each ending type for this topic: *We should do more to help homeless animals.*

MASTER this skill in your workstation.

Ending Techniques

ENDING TYPES—RESTATE THE MAIN IDEA, MAKE A RECOMMEDATION, AND MAKE A PREDICTION

Writing an effective ending is critical for reports, persuasive essays, how-to essays, and literary responses. A good ending will focus the reader's attention by summarizing the discussion or by giving the reader something to think about. Try the three ending techniques described below.

RESTATE THE MAIN IDEA:

So, as you can see, it is our duty to put a stoplight up at the corner of 14th and Main. Only by doing so can we protect the schoolchildren who must cross that street every day.

MAKE A RECOMMENDATION:

To ensure that we get the stoplight we need at 14th and Main, I recommend that every parent and child who crosses that street write a letter to the mayor demanding immediate action.

MAKE A PREDICTION:

If a stoplight isn't installed on 14th and Main soon, it won't be long before someone is seriously injured or possibly killed. Taking action now will prevent such a tragedy.

TASK A	Review some of the topics you have explored in your writer's notebook. Choose at least two of them, and write closings for them that restate the main idea.
TASK B	Make a chart like the one below. Fill in the *Topics* column with some topics you have explored in your writer's notebook. Then, think of a recommendation and a prediction you might use in a closing for each topic. For example:

TOPICS	RECOMMENDATION	PREDICTION
Class sizes	Schools should limit class size to 17 students so that we can get more individual instruction.	If we don't lower class sizes, test scores will stay the same or maybe drop.

TASK C	Review the topic and the opening paragraph of the essay you are currently writing. Write three possible endings, including restating the main idea, making a recommendation, and making a prediction. Place a check next to the ending you think would be the most effective.
TASK D	Select a piece from your draft folder or your notebook that could be improved by revising the ending. Experiment with the different ending types, and rewrite the ending.

Ending Techniques

Mini-lesson

ENDING TYPES—ANSWER A QUESTION, USE A QUOTATION, AND CREATE A SCENARIO

Writing an effective ending is critical for reports, persuasive essays, how-to essays, and literary responses. A good ending will focus the reader's attention by summarizing the discussion or by giving the reader something to think about. Try the three ending techniques described below.

WATCH how it's done. If your essay topic is a report on Abraham Lincoln, you might end in these three different ways:

ANSWER A QUESTION:

When I began this report, I asked, "Which president made the greatest impact on American history?" I think that question has now been answered. For all his important accomplishments and contributions to humanity, Abraham Lincoln stands alone as a man who changed American history forever.

USE A QUOTATION:

In 1863, Lincoln said in his Gettysburg Address that our nation was "dedicated to the proposition that all men are created equal." Not only did he prove that to be true, but he helped make it true. He was a great man.

CREATE A SCENARIO:

Imagine America without Lincoln. America would have splintered into two nations, and millions of souls would have remained in chains for many more years. He saved our nation.

HELP with this example. Think of someone who is very famous today, and then answer the following:

WHAT QUESTION MIGHT THE READER WANT ANSWERED ABOUT THIS PERSON?

WHAT HAS THIS PERSON SAID THAT IS NOTEWORTHY?

HOW WOULD THE WORLD BE DIFFERENT WITHOUT THIS PERSON?

APPLY this skill in your writing notebook. Write for a few minutes about which ending type might apply to your topic. Explain your thinking.

MASTER this skill in your workstation.

Ending Techniques

ENDING TYPES—ANSWER A QUESTION, USE A QUOTATION, AND CREATE A SCENARIO

Writing an effective ending is critical for reports, persuasive essays, how-to essays, and literary responses. A good ending will focus the reader's attention by summarizing the discussion or by giving the reader something to think about. Try the three ending techniques described below.

ANSWER A QUESTION:

When I began this report, I asked, "Which president made the greatest impact on American history?" I think that question has now been answered. For all his important accomplishments and contributions to humanity, Abraham Lincoln stands alone as a man who changed American history forever.

USE A QUOTATION:

In 1863, Lincoln said in his Gettysburg Address that our nation was "dedicated to the proposition that all men are created equal." Not only did he prove that to be true, but he helped make it true. He was a great man.

CREATE A SCENARIO:

Imagine America without Lincoln. America would have splintered into two nations, and millions of souls would have remained in chains for many more years. He saved our nation.

TASK A	**ANSWER A QUESTION:** This ending type is particularly effective when your essay leads with a question. If you chose that lead type, write a conclusion that answers the question that you posed to the reader in the lead of your essay.
TASK B	**USE A QUOTATION:** Gather your research together and use a highlighter to find meaningful quotations that help support your topic. If you are reporting about a person, find a meaningful quote from that person. If you are writing about a subject, try to find a meaningful quote from an expert on that subject. Write a conclusion that includes your quote.
TASK C	**CREATE A SCENARIO:** Write a conclusion that asks your reader to think about the future. Some examples: What would the world be like without the person you are reporting on? How will things get worse if the reader doesn't take your advice? What rewards can the reader expect from following the steps of your how-to essay?
TASK D	Select a piece from your draft folder or your notebook that could be improved by revising the ending. Experiment with the different ending types, and rewrite the ending.

10

Composing Techniques: Target Skill Lessons and Workstation Tasks

Creating Characters

SHOWING THROUGH DESCRIPTION

You can tell your readers what your characters are like, or you can show them! Showing is far more effective. Describing how a character looks as he or she experiences an emotion is an effective way to get your point across and to make sure your reader experiences it, too!

WATCH how it's done.

ORIGINAL SENTENCE:

The baby was cranky.

REVISED WRITING, SHOWING CHARACTER THROUGH DESCRIPTION:

The baby's face scrunched up into a tight little ball, and his tiny fists clenched. His face turned bright red, and he let out a cry that nearly took my ears off.

HELP rewrite this sentence to show character through description.

ORIGINAL SENTENCE:

Lucy was getting really annoyed.

REVISED WRITING, SHOWING CHARACTER THROUGH DESCRIPTION:

APPLY this skill in your writing notebook. Take each of these telling sentences and use description to show how the character looked as he or she experienced the situation in the sentence.

1. Susie wanted that piece of cake.
2. He was afraid of getting caught.
3. She waited anxiously to see if she won the contest.
4. The crowd was joyful when their team won.
5. Boris tried to think of a solution.

MASTER this skill in your workstation.

Creating Characters

SHOWING THROUGH DESCRIPTION

You can tell your readers what your characters are like, or you can show them! Showing is far more effective. Describing how a character looks as he or she experiences an emotion is an effective way to get your point across and to make sure your reader experiences it, too!

ORIGINAL SENTENCE:

The baby was cranky.

REVISED WRITING, SHOWING CHARACTER THROUGH DESCRIPTION:

The baby's face scrunched up into a tight little ball, and his tiny fists clenched. His face turned bright red, and he let out a cry that nearly took my ears off.

TASK A	For each of the following emotions, write a sentence showing how a character might look while experiencing that emotion: amusement, determination, shame, confidence, and fear.
TASK B	Choose two of the emotions listed in Task A, and write a paragraph for each, showing how a character might look while experiencing that emotion. Write complete descriptions to create a picture in your reader's mind.
TASK C	Picture in your mind a time when someone you know experienced a strong emotion. Write a paragraph that completely describes how that person looked as he or she went through that experience.
TASK D	Select a piece from your draft folder or your notebook that could be improved by describing how someone looked as they went through an emotional time. Rewrite that piece by completely describing how the character appeared.

Creating Characters

SHOWING THROUGH ACTION

You can tell your readers what your characters are like, or you can show them! Showing is far more effective. Using action is a great way to let your reader in on what your characters' feelings are. Action gives your characters life and gives your reader a reason to read on!

WATCH how it's done.

ORIGINAL TELLING SENTENCE:

Frank was acting sneaky.

REVISED WRITING, SHOWING CHARACTER THROUGH ACTION:

Frank peered around the corner to see if anyone was coming. He took off his shoes and stood on his tiptoes. He walked gingerly into the room, carefully avoiding the squeaky spots on the wood floor. He breathed in and out so gently that even the dog didn't wake up. At last, when he reached the door, he turned the knob ever so slowly, pulled the door open a few inches, and carefully poked his head into the room.

HELP rewrite this sentence to show action.

ORIGINAL TELLING SENTENCE:

My little sister was cranky.

REVISED WRITING, SHOWING CHARACTER THROUGH ACTION:

APPLY this skill in your writing notebook. Take each of these telling sentences and use action to show what the character is feeling.

1. John was truly happy.
2. Alexa was feeling nervous.
3. The crowd was going wild.
4. My brother loved that little puppy.
5. The teacher was mad at our behavior.

MASTER this skill in your workstation.

Creating Characters

Workstation

SHOWING THROUGH ACTION

You can tell your readers what your characters are like, or you can show them! Showing is far more effective. Using action is a great way to let your reader in on what your characters' feelings are. Action gives your characters life and gives your reader a reason to read on!

ORIGINAL TELLING SENTENCE:

Frank was acting sneaky.

REVISED WRITING, SHOWING CHARACTER THROUGH ACTION:

Frank peered around the corner to see if anyone was coming. He took off his shoes and stood on his tiptoes. He walked gingerly into the room, carefully avoiding the squeaky spots on the wood floor. He breathed in and out so gently that even the dog didn't wake up. At last, when he reached the door, he turned the knob ever so slowly, pulled the door open a few inches, and carefully poked his head into the room.

TASK A   Write an action sentence showing how a character might express each of the following emotions through what he or she does: anger, fear, love, joy, curiosity, boredom, and amazement.

TASK B   Choose two of the emotions listed in Task A, and write a paragraph for each showing how a character might act while feeling that emotion. Write complete descriptions that will let your reader visualize your character's actions.

TASK C   Think of a time when you experienced strong emotions. Write a brief narrative about that time. Don't tell the reader what emotion you're writing about—show the reader! For example, if you're writing about a happy time, don't use the word happy or any synonyms for it (such as joy, delight, etc.). See if you can get the idea across by showing your actions.

TASK D   Select a piece from your draft folder or your notebook that could be improved by adding action to show emotions. Find sentences that tell what a character is feeling, and revise them to show how the character acted at the time he or she experienced those emotions.

Creating Characters

SHOWING THROUGH DIALOGUE

You can tell your readers what your characters are like, or you can show them! Showing is far more effective. Well-developed characters often show what they are like through the things they say. A few choice words of dialogue will make your writing come alive!

WATCH   how it's done.

ORIGINAL SENTENCE:

Regina was disappointed.

REVISED SENTENCE, SHOWING CHARACTER THROUGH DIALOGUE:

"I don't believe it!" Regina cried. "All that work for nothing! I never wanted anything more in my life, and now it's over!"

HELP   with this sentence:

ORIGINAL SENTENCE:

Chester was overjoyed.

REVISED SENTENCE, SHOWING CHARACTER THROUGH DIALOGUE:

APPLY   this skill in your writing notebook. Change each sentence below into dialogue that shows what the character is feeling.

1. My dad was confused.
2. Arthur was hungry.
3. Mimi couldn't believe what she heard.
4. Simon was irritated at his mom.
5. My sister was caring.

MASTER   this skill in your workstation.

Creating Characters

SHOWING THROUGH DIALOGUE

You can tell your readers what your characters are like, or you can show them! Showing is far more effective. Well-developed characters often show what they are like through the things they say. A few choice words of dialogue will make your writing come alive!

ORIGINAL SENTENCE:

Regina was disappointed.

REVISED SENTENCE, SHOWING CHARACTER THROUGH DIALOGUE:

"I don't believe it!" Regina cried. "All that work for nothing! I never wanted anything more in my life, and now it's over!"

TASK A	For each of the following emotions, write a sentence of dialogue showing what a character might say if they were feeling that emotion: delight, concern, depression, sympathy, and pride.
TASK B	Choose two of the emotions listed in Task A, and write several lines of dialogue for each. Using three or four sentences, explore what a character who was going through such emotions might say.
TASK C	Write a dialogue between two characters. Have one character show a strong emotion through dialogue. Pretend that the other character is unaware of what is going on. What would their conversation sound like?
TASK D	Select a piece from your draft folder or your notebook that could be improved by using dialogue to show a character's emotions. Find sentences that tell what a character is feeling, and revise them to show what the character said as he or she experienced the emotions.

Creating Characters

REALISTIC CHARACTERS

In the last few lessons, you've learned how to make characters come alive through description, dialogue, and action. Now it's time to put it all together. Using all three techniques at once can be a powerful tool in your writer's arsenal for creating realistic characters that your readers will want to get to know.

WATCH how it's done.

ORIGINAL SENTENCE:

My mother was worried when my brother still hadn't come home.

REVISED WRITING, SHOWING CHARACTER THROUGH DESCRIPTION, ACTION, AND DIALOGUE:

My mother stared intensely at the clock, watching as each second ticked off. She chewed silently on her fingernails and tapped her foot on the wood floor.

"Where on earth can your brother be?" she asked. "It's two hours past his curfew, and he always calls if he's going to be late."

She reached for the phone and dialed a "9." I knew she was calling the police. Her finger hovered over the "1," but she couldn't push the button.

"No, I can't," she said, bursting into tears. "It's not a police matter. I know it isn't. At least not yet." And she sat back down to resume staring at the clock.

HELP with this sentence. Use description, action, and dialogue to show the emotion the character is feeling:

ORIGINAL SENTENCE:

Simon was happy when he found his lost puppy.

REVISED WRITING, SHOWING CHARACTER THROUGH DESCRIPTION, ACTION, AND DIALOGUE:

APPLY this skill in your writing notebook. Write about an emotional event that happened to someone you know, and describe how that emotion affected that person by describing how they looked at the time, what they said, and what they did.

MASTER this skill in your workstation.

Creating Characters

REALISTIC CHARACTERS

In the last few lessons, you've learned how to make characters come alive through description, dialogue, and action. Now it's time to put it all together. Using all three techniques at once can be a powerful tool in your writer's arsenal for creating realistic characters that your readers will want to get to know.

ORIGINAL SENTENCE:

My mother was worried when my brother still hadn't come home.

REVISED WRITING, SHOWING CHARACTER THROUGH DESCRIPTION, ACTION, AND DIALOGUE:

My mother stared intensely at the clock, watching as each second ticked off. She chewed silently on her fingernails and tapped her foot on the wood floor.

"Where on earth can your brother be?" she asked. "It's two hours past his curfew, and he always calls if he's going to be late."

She reached for the phone and dialed a "9." I knew she was calling the police. Her finger hovered over the "1," but she couldn't push the button.

"No, I can't," she said, bursting into tears. "It's not a police matter. I know it isn't. At least not yet." And she sat back down to resume staring at the clock.

TASK A	For each of the following emotions, write a sentence describing how a person might look, speak, and act while experiencing that emotion: courage, hesitancy, surprise, and impatience.
TASK B	Choose one of the emotions listed in Task A, and develop it into a full description of a character. Fully describe how the character looks, speaks, and acts.
TASK C	Write about a time when you were with someone going through either a very difficult experience or a very joyous experience. Describe this real-life event using all the tools you have learned. Recall the event in your mind, and try to re-create the scene for your reader to make your characters as realistic as possible.
TASK D	Select a piece from your draft folder or your notebook that could be improved by completely describing how a character looked, acted, and spoke. Revise the piece by creating a more fully developed, realistic character.

Point of View

FIRST-PERSON POINT OF VIEW

Point of view refers to who is telling the events. In first-person narration, the events are told exclusively through the eyes of the person discussing the events. First-person narration is perfect for telling true stories, but it can also be used effectively in fictional narratives and essays. First-person pronouns (*I, me, my, mine, we, us, our, ours*) are used throughout, as in "**I** woke up one morning and smelled **my** breakfast cooking." The key is to be consistent—the reader can only know what the person telling the events knows.

WATCH how it's done.

ORIGINAL PARAGRAPH WITH CONFUSING POINT OF VIEW:

I nervously looked at my mom. She was thinking how mad she was and how she'd punish me for disobeying her.

REVISED PARAGRAPH WITH CONSISTENT FIRST-PERSON POINT OF VIEW:

I nervously looked at my mom. I saw her tapping her foot, and I could see from her bulging eyes how mad she was at me. I could only imagine the kind of punishment I was in store for.

HELP with this paragraph. Correct the confusing point of view by rewriting the paragraph in the first person:

ORIGINAL PARAGRAPH WITH CONFUSING POINT OF VIEW:

I went to Sally's birthday party. I was thrilled to be there. She was thinking how great it was to be the center of attention. She was hoping to get a new bike.

REVISED PARAGRAPH WITH CONSISTENT FIRST-PERSON POINT OF VIEW:

APPLY this skill in your writing notebook. Write a brief personal narrative entirely in the first person. Check your work for consistent point of view.

MASTER this skill in your workstation.

Point of View

FIRST-PERSON POINT OF VIEW

Point of view refers to who is telling the events. In first-person narration, the events are told exclusively through the eyes of the person discussing the events. First-person narration is perfect for telling true stories, but it can also be used effectively in fictional narratives and essays. First-person pronouns (*I, me, my, mine, we, us, our, ours*) are used throughout, as in "**I** woke up one morning and smelled **my** breakfast cooking." The key is to be consistent—the reader can only know what the person telling the events knows.

ORIGINAL PARAGRAPH WITH CONFUSING POINT OF VIEW:

I nervously looked at my mom. She was thinking how mad she was and how she'd punish me for disobeying her.

REVISED PARAGRAPH WITH CONSISTENT FIRST-PERSON POINT OF VIEW:

I nervously looked at my mom. I saw her tapping her foot, and I could see from her bulging eyes how mad she was at me. I could only imagine the kind of punishment I was in store for.

TASK A

REPORT: If you're writing an informational report based on personal experiences and/or research you discovered, you should write using the first-person point of view. As you write or review your report, make sure that all of your personal experiences are told in the first person (for example, "When I went to Acapulco last summer, I saw the most beautiful beaches I had ever seen."). Use first-person pronouns throughout (*I, me, my, mine, we, us, our, ours*).

TASK B

PERSUASIVE ESSAY: To write an effective persuasive essay, you should include your personal experiences with the topic, as well as your opinion of the topic. As you write or revise those sections, make sure you are writing in the first person. Use first-person pronouns throughout (*I, me, my, mine, we, us, our, ours*).

TASK C

HOW-TO ESSAY: For how-to or procedural pieces, much of the essay will deal with your own personal experience in accomplishing the task you are explaining to your reader. As you write or revise your how-to essay, make sure you are writing in the first person. Use first-person pronouns throughout (*I, me, my, mine, we, us, our, ours*).

TASK D

NARRATIVE: For narratives, the key to using the first person is consistency. In a fictional narrative, make sure as you write that you only discuss those events that your narrator knows—remember that your narrator can not know what others are thinking. In a personal narrative, you may discuss what you experienced, how you observed others reacting to the events, etc. For either type of narrative, make sure that you use first-person pronouns throughout (*I, me, my, mine, we, us, our, ours*). Look through pieces in your draft folder or your notebook for first-person narration. Correct any inconsistencies.

Point of View

Mini-lesson

LIMITED-OMNISCIENT POINT OF VIEW

Omniscient means "all knowing." In limited-omniscient narration, the author tells the narrative through the eyes of a single character (i.e., we are limited to knowing what that character knows). This type of third-person narration works great in fictional narratives because it brings us inside the mind of a single character—we experience the narrative through the character. The words *he* or *she* are used throughout, as in "**He** crept downstairs and could hear only the sound of **his** own footsteps." The key is to be consistent—the reader can only know what the character knows or can figure out.

WATCH   how it's done. Here's an example of limited-omniscient narration:

He crept downstairs and could hear only the sound of his own footsteps. He knew what his mission was—to get the last piece of chocolate that had been left over from the party. It was dark, but he knew his way to the kitchen well. He grasped the door of the refrigerator and pulled it open. The light from the fridge lit the kitchen, and he suddenly saw the face of his sister, standing there with a smile and a smear of chocolate around her lips.

Notice that we know what the sister did from what the narrator sees, not by anything the sister says or thinks.

HELP   with this sentence starter by completing a paragraph entirely in the point of view of the brother.

Johnny set a fierce smile on his lips and let the ball fly at his sister.

APPLY   this skill in your writing notebook. Write a paragraph of your own using the limited-omniscient point of view. The paragraph can be about anything of your choosing—just make sure that all the actions take place through the eyes of a single character.

MASTER   this skill in your workstation.

Workstation

LIMITED-OMNISCIENT POINT OF VIEW

Omniscient means "all knowing." In limited-omniscient narration, the author tells the narrative through the eyes of a single character (i.e., we are limited to knowing what that character knows). This type of third-person narration works great in fictional narratives because it brings us inside the mind of a single character—we experience the narrative through the character. The words *he* or *she* are used throughout, as in "**He** crept downstairs and could hear only the sound of **his** own footsteps." The key is to be consistent—the reader can only know what the character knows or can figure out.

He crept downstairs and could hear only the sound of his own footsteps. He knew what his mission was—to get the last piece of chocolate that had been left over from the party. It was dark, but he knew his way to the kitchen well. He grasped the door of the refrigerator and pulled it open. The light from the fridge lit the kitchen, and he suddenly saw the face of his sister, standing there with a smile and a smear of chocolate around her lips.

Notice that we know what the sister did from what the narrator sees, not by anything the sister says or thinks.

TASK A

Suppose you are writing a narrative about a character named Carlos, who is going to a sporting event for the first time with his father. What events could we know directly through Carlos's eyes? What could Carlos figure out by observing his father or other people at the event? Copy the chart below and fill it in.

Events Carlos Can Know Directly	What Carlos Can Figure Out
How he feels about being with his father	Whether his father is enjoying the game

---

TASK B

Complete Task A, but take it one step further. Explain **how** Carlos might be able to figure out those things he doesn't know directly. For example, Carlos can figure out whether his father is enjoying the game. He can determine that by what his father says, how his father acts, and his father's facial expressions.

TASK C

Write a paragraph of your own in the limited-omniscient point of view. Write about at least two characters, but let your reader see through the eyes of only one of them.

TASK D

Select a piece from your draft folder or your notebook that is written in the first person. Rewrite some of it using the limited-omniscient point of view. Decide which works better. If you decide to change point of view, work on rewriting your entire piece.

Point of View

OMNISCIENT POINT OF VIEW

Omniscient means "all knowing." In omniscient narration, the author tells the narrative through the eyes of many characters. This type of third-person narration can work well in fictional narratives because it allows us to experience the events of the narrative through many different viewpoints. The narrator can even give us information that none of the characters know. It's almost like watching a movie—the viewer can see everything and hear everything, even things the characters can't see. This type of writing is challenging, however, because the reader must know at all times whose version of the narrative is being told. It is helpful to divide each character's experience by paragraph or section in order to make things clear to the reader.

WATCH how it's done. Here's an example of omniscient narration:

Patrick put the stamp on the letter and smiled. Inside was the ticket to his future, his college admissions application. He had slaved over the essay part for weeks, getting every word right so as to impress the admissions office. Now, it was finished and perfect. And not a moment too soon. He'd have to mail it today to meet the deadline.

Patrick called to his younger sister, Pamela. "Hey, Pam, you pass by the post office on your way to school, don't you? Can you mail this letter for me? It's important."

Pamela took the letter from her brother's hand. "Sure, I'll mail it this morning," she said. Even as she took it, she was fuming because Patrick had gotten her grounded for a week by telling on her the night before. "I'll take care of everything," she said with a wicked smile.

HELP with this example.

Samson was wondering how Mary would react to the news that he would have to break their date. He was nervous, because sometimes Mary could be the sweetest person in the world, but at other times...

"Mary, I've got some bad news for you," said Samson cautiously.

Continue this narrative, showing Mary's thoughts and actions as she learns the news.

APPLY this skill in your writing notebook. Write a paragraph using the omniscient point of view to show what two different characters may think about the same event.

MASTER this skill in your workstation.

Point of View

OMNISCIENT POINT OF VIEW

Omniscient means "all knowing." In omniscient narration, the author tells the narrative through the eyes of many characters. This type of third-person narration can work well in fictional narratives because it allows us to experience the events of the narrative through many different viewpoints. The narrator can even give us information that none of the characters know. It's almost like watching a movie—the viewer can see everything and hear everything, even things the characters can't see. This type of writing is challenging, however, because the reader must know at all times whose version of the narrative is being told. It is helpful to divide each character's experience by paragraph or section in order to make things clear to the reader.

WATCH how it's done. Here's an example of omniscient narration:

Patrick put the stamp on the letter and smiled. Inside was the ticket to his future, his college admissions application. He had slaved over the essay part for weeks, getting every word right so as to impress the admissions office. Now, it was finished and perfect. And not a moment too soon. He'd have to mail it today to meet the deadline.

Patrick called to his younger sister, Pamela. "Hey, Pam, you pass by the post office on your way to school, don't you? Can you mail this letter for me? It's important."

Pamela took the letter from her brother's hand. "Sure, I'll mail it this morning," she said. Even as she took it, she was fuming because Patrick had gotten her grounded for a week by telling on her the night before. "I'll take care of everything," she said with a wicked smile.

TASK A Imagine that a character has won the lottery and calls his friend to tell him. List what each character might say, do, and think about this event.

TASK B Using the situation in Task A, write a scene in which the character tells his friend about winning the lottery. Imagine that the character is joyous, but his friend is jealous and trying to hide his feelings.

TASK C Write a scene of your own in which two or more characters react very differently to the same event. Make sure you include what each character does, says, and thinks about the event.

TASK D Select a piece from your draft folder or your notebook that is written in the first person. Rewrite some of it using the omniscient point of view. Decide which works better. If you decide to change the point of view, work on rewriting your entire piece.

Writing Dialogue

CREDIBLE CONVERSATIONS

Making the conversations between your characters seem credible, or real, is difficult. When your characters talk to each other, is their conversation credible? Will the reader believe that the words you put in quotation marks actually came out of the mouths of real people? If not, it will be hard for the reader to believe the rest of your narrative. Credible conversations allow your reader to connect to your characters.

WATCH how it's done.

ORIGINAL DIALOGUE:

"Hi, Sam."

"Hi, Steve."

"It looks like there's a fire in your room."

"It sure does. We'd better get out of here quick."

"Yes, we should. This could be dangerous."

CREDIBLE DIALOGUE:

"Fire! Fire!" shouted Sam.

"Get out of here now!" Steve cried.

"Wait! I have to save my things! They're gonna be burned up!"

"Are you crazy? You'll die! Get out before it's too late!"

HELP with this dialogue:

ORIGINAL DIALOGUE:

"Ouch! I dropped my bowling ball on my foot," said Tim.

"That looks painful," said John.

"Oh, it certainly is. It's hurting me very much."

"Would you like me to apply some ice to that wound?"

CREDIBLE DIALOGUE:

APPLY this skill in your writing notebook. Ask some questions of a partner. Record his or her exact answers to your questions. Then allow your partner to ask questions of you and record your responses. Write what your partner actually says, even if it's not grammatically correct (most people don't worry too much about grammar in ordinary conversation).

MASTER this skill in your workstation.

Writing Dialogue

CREDIBLE CONVERSATIONS

Making the conversations between your characters seem credible, or real, is difficult. When your characters talk to each other, is their conversation credible? Will the reader believe that the words you put in quotation marks actually came out of the mouths of real people? If not, it will be hard for the reader to believe the rest of your narrative. Credible conversations allow your reader to connect to your characters.

ORIGINAL DIALOGUE:

"Hi, Sam."

"Hi, Steve."

"It looks like there's a fire in your room."

"It sure does. We'd better get out of here quick."

"Yes, we should. This could be dangerous."

CREDIBLE DIALOGUE:

"Fire! Fire!" shouted Sam.

"Get out of here now!" Steve cried.

"Wait! I have to save my things! They're gonna be burned up!"

"Are you crazy? You'll die! Get out before it's too late!"

TASK A   Capture some of the conversations going on around you. Copy down exactly what people say, including their incomplete sentences and whatever slang they may use in informal conversation. After you've captured about ten lines, reflect, in writing, on the differences between conversations (the way people really talk) and formal writing.

TASK B   Choose one of the situations listed below, and write a dialogue between two characters experiencing that situation. Make the dialogue as credible as you can.

1. A person gives the perfect gift to a friend.

2. A teacher reprimands a student for not doing his or her homework.

3. A police officer stops a car for speeding.

TASK C   Create a fictional dialogue between two characters caught in a dramatic situation. Don't use any exposition at all—tell everything through your characters' words.

TASK D   Select a piece from your draft folder or your notebook that could be improved by making the dialogue more credible. Revise your writing so that the conversation seems genuine.

Writing Dialogue

"SAID" STOPPERS

Using the word *said* too often in your dialogue gets boring—fast! Spice up your dialogue using words other than *said*. Characters can *reply, state, mumble, shout, respond*—the number of words you can use is surprisingly large. Match the words you use to describe dialogue to the emotion of the character's words. An angry person would **yell**, but not **whisper**. Also, remember that in dialogue between two people, it isn't necessary to use a *said* word after each line. Since the speakers are taking turns, the reader knows who is speaking by whose turn it is.

WATCH how it's done.

ORIGINAL DIALOGUE, USING SAID:

"I'm really getting angry," I said.

"Really? I couldn't tell by your red face," she said.

"Stop it!" I said.

"You stop looking like a tomato first," she said.

REVISED DIALOGUE, USING WORDS OTHER THAN SAID:

"I'm really getting angry," I growled.

"Really? I couldn't tell by your red face," she teased.

"Stop it!"

"You stop looking like a tomato first," she laughed.

HELP with this dialogue:

ORIGINAL DIALOGUE, USING SAID:

"I'm so late! What time is it?" I said.

"Oh my. It's 6 o'clock. You really are late," she said.

"What am I going to do?" I said.

"I'd hurry up if I were you," she said.

REVISED DIALOGUE, USING WORDS OTHER THAN SAID:

APPLY this skill in your writing notebook. Write ten lines of dialogue. Try to use the word *said* no more than one time.

MASTER this skill in your workstation.

Writing Dialogue

"SAID" STOPPERS

Using the word *said* too often in your dialogue gets boring—fast! Spice up your dialogue using words other than *said*. Characters can *reply, state, mumble, shout, respond*—the number of words you can use is surprisingly large. Match the words you use to describe dialogue to the emotion of the character's words. An angry person would **yell**, but not **whisper**. Also, remember that in dialogue between two people, it isn't necessary to use a *said* word after each line. Since the speakers are taking turns, the reader knows who is speaking by whose turn it is.

ORIGINAL DIALOGUE, USING SAID:

"I'm really getting angry," I said.

"Really? I couldn't tell by your red face," she said.

"Stop it!" I said.

"You stop looking like a tomato first," she said.

REVISED DIALOGUE, USING WORDS OTHER THAN SAID:

"I'm really getting angry," I growled.

"Really? I couldn't tell by your red face," she teased.

"Stop it!"

"You stop looking like a tomato first," she laughed.

TASK A	Go through your reading book, and record as many *other-than-said* words as you can find. Make a list for yourself to use in the future.
TASK B	Write two lines of dialogue for each of the following emotions: joy, sorrow, fear, anger, disgust. Use *other-than-said* words that match the emotion in your dialogue. For example, if the emotion is love, you might write *"You've got the cutest eyes," she cooed.*
TASK C	Write an imaginary dialogue between two people who are having an argument. In the first five lines of dialogue, have the characters speak angrily with each other. In the last five lines, have them begin to make up. Remember that in dialogue between two people, it isn't necessary to point out who is speaking in every line.
TASK D	Select a piece from your draft folder or your notebook that could be improved by changing some *other-than-said* words in the dialogue or by eliminating such words from dialogue where it's already clear who is speaking.

Writing the Body   # Mini-lesson

THE FIVE Ws OF NARRATIVES

Basic to any narrative is including the five Ws: who, what, where, when, and why. *Who* tells you the character(s); *what* tells you the events that happened (the plot); *when* and *where* tell you the setting; and *why* explains the reason the events took place. Knowing these details before you begin to write will help you create a solid plot.

WATCH   how it's done.

ORIGINAL NARRATIVE IDEA:

The day we adopted a dog

IDEA PLUS THE FIVE Ws:

Who: My father, my mother, my sister, and myself

What (happened): We went to the shelter to adopt a dog

Where: The Wagging Tail Dog Shelter

When: Two months ago, in early July

Why: My parents thought we needed to learn responsibility

HELP   with this narrative idea. Add the five Ws to begin creating a plot:

ORIGINAL NARRATIVE IDEA:

The day I left the water running in the tub

IDEA PLUS THE FIVE Ws:

Who:

What:

Where:

When:

Why:

APPLY   this skill in your writing notebook. Think of an event that happened to you or someone you know, and write out the five Ws of that event.

MASTER   this skill in your workstation.

Writing the Body

THE FIVE Ws OF NARRATIVES

Basic to any narrative is including the five Ws: who, what, where, when, and why. *Who* tells you the character(s); *what* tells you the events that happened (the plot); *when* and *where* tell you the setting; and *why* explains the reason the events took place. Knowing these details before you begin to write will help you create a solid plot.

ORIGINAL NARRATIVE IDEA:

The day we adopted a dog

IDEA PLUS THE FIVE Ws:

Who: My father, my mother, my sister, and myself

What (happened): We went to the shelter to adopt a dog

Where: The Wagging Tail Dog Shelter

When: Two months ago, in early July

Why: My parents thought we needed to learn responsibility

TASK A   Create a chart like the one below in your notebook. Fill in all the *who* lines with your own name and the names of other people you are close with. Then, begin to fill in the other lines using narratives you know about these people.

WHO	WHAT	WHERE	WHEN	WHY
Myself				

TASK B   Choose one of the five W narratives you charted in Task A, and begin to write in some details for each W. For example:

Who: Myself, when I was twelve years old

What: I got myself in trouble by knocking my mom's favorite dishes on the floor

Where: The kitchen in my house, up on a shelf that I was never supposed to touch

---

TASK C   Think of an event that happened to you that might make an interesting narrative. Write out the five Ws for the narrative, and then start writing the narrative in your notebook.

TASK D   Select a piece from your draft folder or your notebook. Review the piece, and write out the five Ws of your piece. If anything is missing, add it in. If needed, add details to each of the five Ws. Then, add those details to your piece.

Writing the Body

THE FIVE Ws OF NON-FICTION

Newspaper reporters know they must tell their readers the five Ws of any narrative—the *who, what, where, when,* and *why.* You can adapt that approach to your own non-fiction writing to make sure you've given the reader all the important details of your topic.

WATCH how it's done. If you're writing about a famous person, for example, the reader will want to know certain facts.

Who the person is

What happened in this person's life

Where the person lived

When the person was alive

Why this person is noteworthy today

HELP with this topic. Suppose you are reporting on your school's principal. Fill in the five Ws.

WHO:

WHAT:

WHERE:

WHEN:

WHY:

APPLY this skill in your writing notebook. Think of a person you know well, and write out the five Ws for that person. Then think of a topic you know well, and write out the five Ws for that topic.

MASTER this skill in your workstation.

Writing the Body

Workstation

THE FIVE Ws OF NON-FICTION

Newspaper reporters know they must tell their readers the five Ws of any narrative—the *who*, *what*, *where*, *when*, and *why*. You can adapt that approach to your own non-fiction writing to make sure you've given the reader all the important details of your topic.

TASK A REPORT: Write out the five Ws of your report topic. Keep in mind that there may be more than one person or place involved.

TASK B PERSUASIVE ESSAY: Write out the five Ws for your persuasive essay. Keep in mind that in persuasion, your Ws will be a little different. Follow the format below and answer the question for each W:

What is the problem and your proposed solution?

Why is this a problem?

Who is affected by this problem?

Where is this a problem? (Local, national, worldwide)

When did this problem begin?

TASK C HOW-TO ESSAY: In how-to writing, your five Ws should address the concerns of the reader attempting to follow your directions. They should look something like this:

What is the task being explained?

Why should someone attempt this task?

Who can do this task?

Where can this task be done?

When should this task be done?

TASK D LITERARY RESPONSE: Your five Ws will depend on whether you are discussing an author or a genre.

If you're discussing an author, discuss **who** the author is, **what** the author has written, **when** and **where** the author lived, and **why** someone might want to read this author.

If you're discussing a genre, discuss **what** the genre is, **who** some famous authors in that genre are, **when** and **where** the genre gained popularity, and **why** the genre should be of interest to readers.

Now write out the five Ws for your literary response.

Writing the Body

CPR—CHARACTER, PROBLEM, RESOLUTION

Sure, you've heard of giving a person CPR to keep them alive, but good writing needs CPR to be born! CPR stands for *character*, *problem*, and *resolution*—the three most basic elements that every narrative must have. Once you've figured out the CPR of your narrative, you can fill it in with more details to help create your plot—the events of your narrative.

WATCH how it's done.

> CHARACTER: Joe, a new student in school
> PROBLEM: He's getting bullied because he's new
> RESOLUTION: He stands up to the bully and gains the respect of his classmates

As you can see, this is the "bare bones" of a narrative, but once you've done your CPR, you can fill in the details as you write.

HELP with this narrative. Decide on a problem and a resolution that would fit in with this character:

> CHARACTER: Cynthia, who just arrived in a new city
> PROBLEM:
>
>
>
>
> RESOLUTION:

APPLY this skill in your writing notebook. Create several CPRs that you might want to use in a future narrative. Remember, every narrative contains a character with a problem that must be resolved one way or another by the end of the narrative. Writing CPRs is a great way to get ideas for future writing projects!

MASTER this skill in your workstation.

Writing the Body

CPR—CHARACTER, PROBLEM, RESOLUTION

Sure, you've heard of giving a person CPR to keep them alive, but good writing needs CPR to be born! CPR stands for *character*, *problem*, and *resolution*—the three most basic elements that every narrative must have. Once you've figured out the CPR of your narrative, you can fill it in with more details to help create your plot—the events of your narrative.

CHARACTER: Joe, a new student in school

PROBLEM: He's getting bullied because he's new

RESOLUTION: He stands up to the bully and gains the respect of his classmates

As you can see, this is the "bare bones" of a narrative, but once you've done your CPR, you can fill in the details as you write.

TASK A Flip through your notebook and review some of the narratives you've written. On a sticky note, write down the CPR for each narrative, and attach it to the narrative.

TASK B For each of the characters listed below, think of a problem and resolution that the character might have in a narrative.

Character 1: Antonio, a young boy who wants to be like his older brother

Character 2: Elena, a teenage girl with a crush on a classmate

Character 3: Simone, a young woman entering college

TASK C Write as many CPRs as you can, using people you really know as your characters. You may write about real problems they actually faced, or you may create fictional problems for them to confront.

TASK D Use a CPR that you created to write a notebook piece that may develop into a future narrative. Begin to fill in some of the details of your character's life and problems as you write.

Writing the Body

CONFLICT

Every narrative revolves around a conflict, or a problem that a character must face. Conflicts drive the action in your narrative, so presenting your character with a challenging conflict is key to an engaging story.

WATCH how it's done.

ORIGINAL NARRATIVE WITHOUT A CONFLICT:

My brother's birthday party was wonderful. I gave him a great present, and he had a wonderful time.

Notice how the writer has nowhere to go with this narrative because there is no conflict. Nothing happens or can happen in this type of narrative until a conflict arises. Add a conflict and things begin to take shape:

REVISED NARRATIVE WITH A CONFLICT:

My brother's birthday party was wonderful. Everyone gave him great presents. I couldn't wait to see the look on his face when he opened the baseball glove I bought him. The only problem was that I noticed, far off in the corner of the room, my dog hungrily chewing the glove to bits.

HELP with this narrative. Add a conflict to the situation that will grip the reader's interest:

ORIGINAL NARRATIVE WITHOUT A CONFLICT:

My first day in my new school was exciting. There were many new faces, and a lot of people smiled at me.

REVISED NARRATIVE WITH A CONFLICT:

APPLY this skill in your writing notebook. Think of a conflict or problem that could arise in each of the following situations:

1. A family vacation
2. A major test in school
3. Making a new friend
4. Moving to a new home
5. A sporting event

MASTER this skill in your workstation.

Writing the Body

Workstation

CONFLICT

Every narrative revolves around a conflict, or a problem that a character must face. Conflicts drive the action in your narrative, so presenting your character with a challenging conflict is key to an engaging story.

ORIGINAL NARRATIVE WITHOUT A CONFLICT:

My brother's birthday party was wonderful. I gave him a great present, and he had a wonderful time.

Notice how the writer has nowhere to go with this narrative because there is no conflict. Nothing happens or can happen in this type of narrative until a conflict arises. Add a conflict and things begin to take shape:

REVISED NARRATIVE WITH A CONFLICT:

My brother's birthday party was wonderful. Everyone gave him great presents. I couldn't wait to see the look on his face when he opened the baseball glove I bought him. The only problem was that I noticed, far off in the corner of the room, my dog hungrily chewing the glove to bits.

TASK A Conflicts often arise in new situations. Make a list of new situations that a person can experience, and write down a conflict that might arise in that situation. For example:

NEW SITUATION
Moving to a new city

CONFLICT
Not having any friends and feeling lonely

TASK B Make a list of conflicts or problems that you've actually experienced in your life. They may be problems that you faced personally or challenges that happened to people you know.

TASK C Write about a conflict that you've actually experienced or a conflict that has happened to someone you know. Write a one-page narrative about the conflict, telling the situation, the people involved, the problem they faced, and how the problem was solved.

TASK D Select a piece from your draft folder or your notebook that could be improved by either adding a conflict or making the conflict clearer to the reader. Revise the piece.

NARRATIVE SIGNIFICANCE

How much thought do you put into the significance, or meaning, of your narratives? If all you concern yourself with is making sure you complete an assignment, your narrative probably won't be very interesting! Most readers read for a reason—to learn something, to experience something they haven't personally experienced, or to gather information. Most creative writing focuses on teaching a lesson of some sort. Your characters should learn something through their experiences. If they don't, what was the point of telling your narrative? Before you begin to write, make sure you know what the significance of your narrative will be.

WATCH how it's done.

ORIGINAL NARRATIVE WITHOUT SIGNIFICANCE:

I want to tell you all about the time we went to the amusement park. It was one of the most fun times I ever had! I can't wait to go back. Let me tell you all about it.

REVISED NARRATIVE WITH SIGNIFICANCE:

I went to the amusement park to have a day of fun. And it was fun—until I almost got hurt on one of the rides. It might have been worse if my aunt hadn't saved me from the dreaded Stomach Turner ride. I didn't realize how much my loved ones would risk to protect me, but I found out that day and had a great time afterwards. Here's what happened.

HELP with this narrative:

ORIGINAL NARRATIVE WITHOUT SIGNIFICANCE:

I was miserable the day I lost fifty dollars. I thought it would be the end of the world and that my parents would kill me. I was totally depressed.

What significance might be written into this narrative? Help continue the narrative to include its significance:

REVISED NARRATIVE WITH SIGNIFICANCE:

APPLY this skill in your writing notebook. Make a list of lessons you've learned in your life. Pick one or two that you think might make good narratives, and write down some of the events that helped you learn those lessons.

MASTER this skill in your workstation.

Writing the Body

NARRATIVE SIGNIFICANCE

How much thought do you put into the significance, or meaning, of your narratives? If all you concern yourself with is making sure you complete an assignment, your narrative probably won't be very interesting! Most readers read for a reason—to learn something, to experience something they haven't personally experienced, or to gather information. Most creative writing focuses on teaching a lesson of some sort. Your characters should learn something through their experiences. If they don't, what was the point of telling your narrative? Before you begin to write, make sure you know what the significance of your narrative will be.

ORIGINAL NARRATIVE WITHOUT SIGNIFICANCE:

I want to tell you all about the time we went to the amusement park. It was one of the most fun times I ever had! I can't wait to go back. Let me tell you all about it.

REVISED NARRATIVE WITH SIGNIFICANCE:

I went to the amusement park to have a day of fun. And it was fun—until I almost got hurt on one of the rides. It might have been worse if my aunt hadn't saved me from the dreaded Stomach Turner ride. I didn't realize how much my loved ones would risk to protect me, but I found out that day and had a great time afterwards. Here's what happened.

TASK A	Make a list of some of the lessons learned by the characters in books and narratives that you've read. Reflect on these lessons, and put a check next to any that you think you might be able to use in a future narrative.

TASK B	Reflect on a recent book you've read or on a TV show or a movie you've seen. What was the lesson of the narrative? Once you've identified the lesson, reflect in writing on how the narrative made the lesson clear. How did the characters learn the lesson they learned?

TASK C	Write about a time that you learned an important lesson. If you've done Task B, you may want to choose one of those lessons for your narrative. Describe the situation, but don't tell the lesson! When you're finished, read your narrative to a partner and see if he or she can figure out the lesson from the narrative you've told. If he or she can, you did a great job!

TASK D	Select a piece from your draft folder or your notebook that could be improved by focusing on the significance of the narrative. Rather than simply telling the reader what the lesson of your narrative is, work on making the lesson clear through the events and dialogue you include.

Mini-lesson

FLASHBACKS

Most narratives are told in time order, and the reason is simple: It helps the reader see the events of a narrative unfold just as they happened. Sometimes, however, it is useful to use a flashback in your narrative. A flashback is when an author takes the narrative out of time sequence to an earlier time. Sometimes this is done to explain events, to analyze a character's thoughts, or to help create suspense. Using this technique can be effective, but it can also be tricky because it must be made very clear to the reader when the narrative goes back in time and when it returns to the present. You'll find that flashbacks can be very entertaining when they're done right!

WATCH how it's done. Notice how the first sentence helps indicate to the reader that a flashback is about to occur and how the last sentence signals that the flashback is over:

Joe tried to remember the last time he'd seen his long-lost cousin, and then he remembered.

It was twelve years ago on a dark autumn night. Joe had been playing ball and having a blast when he felt a tap on his shoulder. It was his cousin Winston. He whispered in Joe's ear, "Hey, champ. Promise that you'll always remember me, no matter what happens, OK?" Joe remembered feeling strange hearing those words, as if something terrible were about to happen. But he didn't know what.

Those words seemed to haunt him now as he pondered what ever became of his cousin.

HELP with this example. Write a flashback that might follow the sentence below. End the flashback with a sentence that brings the reader back to the present:

It seemed to Sally that she had heard that voice before.

APPLY this skill in your writing notebook. Write a flashback that might follow this sentence: *There was only one other time in her life when Sue was as happy as she felt now.*

MASTER this skill in your workstation.

Writing the Body

FLASHBACKS

Most narratives are told in time order, and the reason is simple: It helps the reader see the events of a narrative unfold just as they happened. Sometimes, however, it is useful to use a flashback in your narrative. A flashback is when an author takes the narrative out of time sequence to an earlier time. Sometimes this is done to explain events, to analyze a character's thoughts, or to help create suspense. Using this technique can be effective, but it can also be tricky because it must be made very clear to the reader when the narrative goes back in time and when it returns to the present. You'll find that flashbacks can be very entertaining when they're done right!

Notice how the first sentence helps indicate to the reader that a flashback is about to occur and how the last sentence signals that the flashback is over:

Joe tried to remember the last time he'd seen his long-lost cousin, and then he remembered.

It was twelve years ago on a dark autumn night. Joe had been playing ball and having a blast when he felt a tap on his shoulder. It was his cousin Winston. He whispered in Joe's ear, "Hey, champ. Promise that you'll always remember me, no matter what happens, OK?" Joe remembered feeling strange hearing those words, as if something terrible were about to happen. But he didn't know what.

Those words seemed to haunt him now as he pondered what ever became of his cousin.

TASK A   Write a possible flashback for each of these sentences:

1. Steven wondered where he had seen that face before.
2. Samantha tried to remember the last time she had a good time at her grandmother's house.

TASK B   Write a possible flashback for each of these sentences. Then, write an additional paragraph that brings the reader back into the present.

1. Maira had a strange feeling that she had visited this town before.
2. Josephine wanted things to be good again, like they were when she was back in grade school.

TASK C   Create a sentence of your own that introduces a flashback (see examples of these types of sentences in Tasks A and B above). Then write the flashback itself. Finish up by writing a sentence or two that brings the reader back to the present.

TASK D   Select a piece from your draft folder or your notebook that could be improved through the use of flashback. Make sure you clearly introduce the flashback so the reader knows it is about to occur, and conclude the flashback by bringing the reader back to the present.

Writing the Body

Mini-lesson

SUSPENSE

Suspense creates a feeling of tension in your narrative, and it's what makes the reader want to keep on reading. While suspense may make you think of scary stories, most types of narratives rely on suspense to propel the reader forward. Suspense can be created by telling the reader some, but not all, of what is to come. Suspense also relies on mood, setting, and characters to be effective, so don't forget to work on those as you slowly unravel your narrative for the reader.

WATCH   how it's done.

ORIGINAL PARAGRAPH:

I'll never forget the day I lost my dog. We spent hours and hours searching for him. I thought we'd never get him back! I was so relieved when we finally found him. Here's what happened that day.

Notice that the above paragraph has already given away the narrative so that the reader has no real reason to continue. Create suspense by holding some details back:

REVISED PARAGRAPH, WITH SUSPENSE:

I'll never forget the day I lost my dog. My mom wanted to kill me for being so careless. My dad spent four hours searching under cars and in back alleys. If they didn't find him, I'd be in hot water for months. I never had such a miserable day.

HELP   with this paragraph. Rewrite it so that it is more suspenseful:

ORIGINAL PARAGRAPH:

My trip to the local "haunted" house was very scary. I started out thinking I would meet a ghost, but as it turned out, it was an ordinary old house after all. Let me tell you about it.

REVISED PARAGRAPH, WITH SUSPENSE:

APPLY   this skill in your writing notebook. Write the beginning paragraph(s) of a narrative, and include suspense. Hold some details of the narrative back from your readers to make them want to read on.

MASTER   this skill in your workstation.

Writing the Body

SUSPENSE

Suspense creates a feeling of tension in your narrative, and it's what makes the reader want to keep on reading. While suspense may make you think of scary stories, most types of narratives rely on suspense to propel the reader forward. Suspense can be created by telling the reader some, but not all, of what is to come. Suspense also relies on mood, setting, and characters to be effective, so don't forget to work on those as you slowly unravel your narrative for the reader.

ORIGINAL PARAGRAPH:

I'll never forget the day I lost my dog. We spent hours and hours searching for him. I thought we'd never get him back! I was so relieved when we finally found him. Here's what happened that day.

Notice that the above paragraph has already given away the narrative so that the reader has no real reason to continue. Create suspense by holding some details back:

REVISED PARAGRAPH, WITH SUSPENSE:

I'll never forget the day I lost my dog. My mom wanted to kill me for being so careless. My dad spent four hours searching under cars and in back alleys. If they didn't find him, I'd be in hot water for months. I never had such a miserable day.

TASK A The following paragraph gives away the entire narrative and completely lacks suspense. Rewrite the paragraph to make it more suspenseful.

My cousin's birthday party was a great success. We had planned it for weeks. It was a surprise party, but the surprise was on us because my cousin discovered our plan the day before the party! Let me tell you what happened.

TASK B Think of an event in your life that was suspenseful in some way. Then, make a list of the events that make up the narrative. When you are done, place a check next to each event you could tell early on in the narrative, and an X next to those events that should be told later to create suspense.

TASK C Write a suspenseful narrative in your notebook. Make sure that you tell only what the reader has to know at first. You may also want to experiment with creating a setting, mood, or characters that fit in with your suspenseful narrative.

TASK D Select a piece from your draft folder or your notebook that could be improved by adding suspense. Look for places where you give away too much information, and plan where you can place those events instead to create greater suspense.

Writing the Body

Mini-lesson

SETTING THE MOOD

Mood is the feeling expressed in a piece of writing. If you're writing a narrative about a happy event, for example, the people, places, events, and discussions should reflect that happiness. If you're writing a report on the importance of volunteering, you may want to give your piece a feeling of hope. Giving your writing a sense of mood helps the reader feel what you want him/her to experience.

WATCH how it's done.

ORIGINAL SENTENCE:

My birthday was a really happy day.

REVISED WRITING, SETTING THE MOOD:

Colorful balloons and ribbons were hung everywhere. There was the sound of everyone laughing and chatting away. My mom smiled as she led me to the huge mound of presents, all carefully wrapped in festive paper. I couldn't help smiling. "Mom," I said, "This is the happiest day of my life!"

HELP with this example. If you were writing a report on some soldiers gathering for the twentieth anniversary of the day they lost some fellow soldiers in battle, you would try to create a mood of seriousness and sadness. Think how you might describe the people and the place. What might take place? What might be said by the soldiers to help express the mood?

ORIGINAL SENTENCE:

The soldiers marched down the street, slowly stepping to the beat of a solitary drum.

REVISED WRITING, SETTING THE MOOD:

APPLY this skill in your writing notebook. Write a paragraph or two that set the mood for this sentence: *My hometown is the most exciting place I know.*

MASTER this skill in your workstation.

Writing the Body

Workstation

SETTING THE MOOD

Mood is the feeling expressed in a piece of writing. If you're writing a narrative about a happy event, for example, the people, places, events, and discussions should reflect that happiness. If you're writing a report on the importance of volunteering, you may want to give your piece a feeling of hope. Giving your writing a sense of mood helps the reader feel what you want him/her to experience.

ORIGINAL SENTENCE:

My birthday was a really happy day.

REVISED WRITING, SETTING THE MOOD:

Colorful balloons and ribbons were hung everywhere. There was the sound of everyone laughing and chatting away. My mom smiled as she led me to the huge mound of presents, all carefully wrapped in festive paper. I couldn't help smiling. "Mom," I said, "This is the happiest day of my life!"

TASK A   Think of a situation in your life that created a certain mood in you. Write about that situation, and try to get the mood across to your reader through the characters and their actions, as well as the setting and dialogue.

TASK B   For each of the writing topics listed below, tell what the mood might be. Then note the types of people, places, events, and discussions that might be included.

1. Aliens land on earth.

2. Someone wins the lottery.

3. Your school needs more money for basic supplies.

4. America is a great country.

TASK C   Review the situations given in Task B. Choose one, and write several paragraphs that express the mood of the situation. Be sure to describe the people, places, events, and discussions that help express the mood in your paragraphs.

TASK D   Select a piece from your draft folder or your notebook that could be improved by setting the mood. Revise descriptions of people, places, and events to express the mood.

Composing Techniques: Target Skill Lessons and Workstation Tasks

Writing the Body

Mini-lesson

COMPARE/CONTRAST

To compare is to show how things are the same, and to contrast is to show how they are different. An excellent way to start is to use a Venn diagram like the one below. A Venn diagram consists of two overlapping circles. Information in the overlapping part shows what is the same, and the rest shows what is different.

WATCH how it's done. This Venn diagram compares and contrasts computers of different eras:

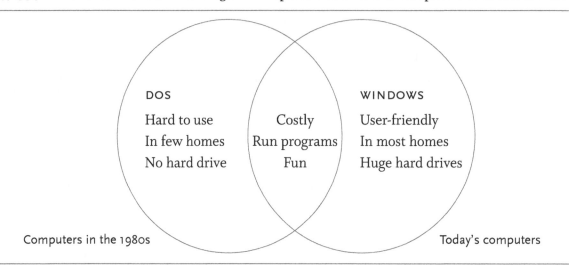

DOS

Hard to use
In few homes
No hard drive

Costly
Run programs
Fun

WINDOWS

User-friendly
In most homes
Huge hard drives

Computers in the 1980s   Today's computers

HELP with this Venn diagram. The topic is the difference between elementary schools and middle schools.

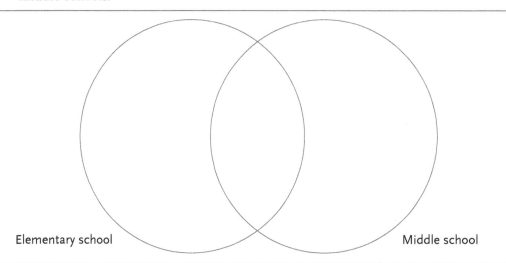

Elementary school   Middle school

APPLY this skill in your writing notebook. Use a Venn diagram to compare and contrast two people you know outside this class. You may use famous people if you wish.

MASTER this skill in your workstation.

Writing the Body

Workstation

COMPARE/CONTRAST

To compare is to show how things are the same, and to contrast is to show how they are different. An excellent way to start is to use a Venn diagram like the one below. A Venn diagram consists of two overlapping circles. Information in the overlapping part shows what is the same, and the rest shows what is different.

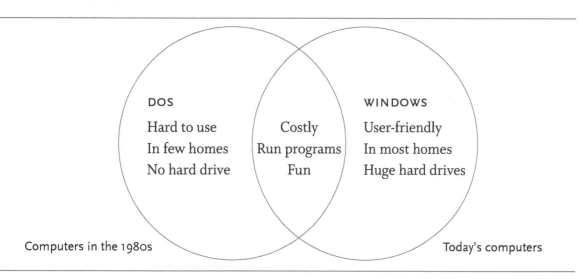

TASK A

REPORTS: Create a Venn diagram comparing and contrasting your topic. If your topic is
- A famous person—compare that person to someone else like him or her. For example, compare presidents, ball players, famous figures in history, etc.
- A place—compare the place to where you currently live.
- A thing—compare it to something similar. For example, if you're reporting on cars, compare two similar models.

When you are done, write a paragraph using the information from your Venn diagram.

TASK B

PERSUASIVE ESSAYS: Create a Venn diagram comparing and contrasting the two opposing points of view on your topic. For example, if you were trying to persuade your principal to reduce homework, your Venn diagram would show how things are now, and how they would be with less homework. When you are done, write a paragraph using the information from your Venn diagram to persuade your reader.

TASK C

HOW-TO ESSAYS: Create a Venn diagram comparing and contrasting two different ways of doing the same task. When you are done, write a paragraph using the information from your Venn diagram that shows why one method of doing things is better than the other.

TASK D

LITERARY RESPONSES: Create a Venn diagram comparing and contrasting literary characters, authors, themes, or genres. When you are done, write a paragraph using the information from your Venn diagram discussing which character, author, theme, or genre you like better and why.

Word Choice

Mini-lesson

CHOOSING STRONG WORDS

No matter what genre you happen to be writing in, readers judge your writing by the words you select. Strong words are more specific, descriptive, or convincing than more ordinary words. By choosing strong words, you give power to your message. Try it, and see how just a few changes in word choice can make a difference!

WATCH how it's done. See how strong words can be added and how some of the weak words in the original paragraph can be changed to make a much stronger paragraph.

ORIGINAL PARAGRAPH:

It makes sense to ask your parents permission before you hold a party in your house. If you don't, you can get into trouble. Your parents will be upset. You may find that they'll say yes if you ask permission. So it's better to ask than to be sorry later.

REVISED PARAGRAPH WITH STRONG WORDS

Clearly, it makes sense to ask your parents' permission prior to holding a party in your house. If you don't, you will **undoubtedly** get into trouble. Your parents will be **understandably** upset if you don't ask. **Conversely**, you may find that they'll say yes if you ask their permission. **Simply put**, it's better to ask than to be sorry later.

HELP with these examples. Using the **Strong Words for Essay Writing** sheet, write a sentence containing each type of strong word. For example:

PERSUASIVE WORDS:

This is **undoubtedly** the best solution.

Time Order:

Cause and Effect:

Compare/contrast:

Absolute Words:

Summary Words:

APPLY this skill in your writing notebook. Write at least ten sentences of your own using the words from the **Strong Words for Essay Writing** sheet.

MASTER this skill in your workstation.

Word Choice

Workstation

CHOOSING STRONG WORDS

No matter what genre you happen to be writing in, readers judge your writing by the words you select. Strong words are more specific, descriptive, or convincing than more ordinary words. By choosing strong words, you give power to your message. Try it, and see how just a few changes in word choice can make a difference!

ORIGINAL PARAGRAPH:

It makes sense to ask your parents permission before you hold a party in your house. If you don't, you can get into trouble. Your parents will be upset. You may find that they'll say yes if you ask permission. So it's better to ask than to be sorry later.

REVISED PARAGRAPH WITH STRONG WORDS

Clearly, it makes sense to ask your parents' permission prior to holding a party in your house. If you don't, you will **undoubtedly** get into trouble. Your parents will be **understandably** upset if you don't ask. **Conversely**, you may find that they'll say yes if you ask their permission. **Simply put**, it's better to ask than to be sorry later.

TASK A   REPORTS: Revise your report with words from the **Strong Words for Essay Writing** sheet. Use a summary word in your conclusion. Use the **Strong Words for Descriptive Writing** sheet to make your descriptions more powerful.

TASK B   PERSUASIVE ESSAYS: First, revise your writing with words from the "Persuasive Words" section of the **Strong Words for Essay Writing** sheet. Then, decide what other strong words you might be able to use (cause/effect and compare/contrast words are often found in persuasive writing, so check those words to determine if there are any you can use). Use one of the summary words in your conclusion.

TASK C   HOW-TO ESSAYS: First, revise your writing with words from the "Time-Order Words" section of the **Strong Words for Essay Writing** sheet. Then, decide what other strong words you might be able to use (cause/effect is often used in how-to writing, so check those words to determine if there are any you can use). Use one of the summary words in your conclusion.

TASK D   NARRTIVES OR LITERARY RESPONSES: Revise your writing by focusing on choosing strong words in your descriptions. The **Strong Words for Descriptive Writing** sheet may help you. If you're writing a literary response, also work on revising your expository writing with the **Strong Words for Essay Writing** sheet.

Strong Words for Essay Writing

PERSUASIVE WORDS

appropriately
certainly
clearly
conclusively
logically
not surprisingly
obviously
rationally
understandably
undoubtedly
unquestionable
without question

TIME-ORDER WORDS

afterwards
at the onset
eventually
firstly
in conclusion
initially
lastly
meanwhile
originally
presently
previously
ultimately

CAUSE-AND-EFFECT WORDS

accordingly
as a result
consequently
hence
in consequence
inasmuch as
resultantly
subsequently
therefore
thus

SUMMARY WORDS

accordingly
as expected
briefly
for these reasons
in conclusion
in review
in short
in summation
inasmuch as
on the whole
simply put
therefore
thus

ABSOLUTE WORDS

absolutely
always
eternally
everlastingly
for evermore
forever
infinitely
invariably
never
nevermore
permanently
perpetually
positively
without exception

COMPARE/CONTRAST WORDS

alternately
comparably
contrastingly
conversely
correspondingly
equivalent
identically
in opposition
likewise
on the other hand
separately
similarly
vice versa

Strong Words for Descriptive Writing

NICE	GOOD	BAD
becoming	excellent	abominable
delightful	exceptional	atrocious
lovely	marvelous	dreadful
pleasant	satisfying	imperfect
splendid	tip-top	lousy
superior	top notch	substandard
winning	wonderful	unsatisfactory

BEAUTIFUL	UGLY	BIG
alluring	deformed	colossal
bewitching	grotesque	enormous
dazzling	hideous	gigantic
exquisite	loathsome	hulking
radiant	repulsive	massive
ravishing	revolting	prodigious
sublime	unsightly	voluminous

SMALL	COLORFUL	EXCITING
diminutive	brilliant	astonishing
meager	flashy	dramatic
microscopic	gaudy	electrifying
minuscule	multicolored	exhilarating
paltry	prismatic	eye-popping
puny	vibrant	stirring
tiny	vivid	thrilling

HAPPY	SAD	KIND
cheerful	bereaved	amiable
delighted	despairing	benevolent
ecstatic	despondent	charitable
elated	grief-stricken	compassionate
joyous	heartsick	generous
jubilant	melancholy	sympathetic
thrilled	sorrowful	tender-hearted

Word Choice

Mini-lesson

VIVID VERBS

Verbs are action words, and choosing the right ones can make your writing soar! Every sentence contains at least one verb, so make sure that yours make an impact on your readers by choosing vivid verbs that help describe the mood and feeling in your writing.

WATCH how it's done. Here's a paragraph with verbs that fail to communicate feeling to the reader (verbs are underlined):

ORIGINAL PARAGRAPH:

Tears <u>ran</u> from her eyes. Her face <u>turned</u> red. She <u>breathed</u> loudly, and she <u>inhaled</u> as if she couldn't <u>get</u> enough air. She <u>put</u> her head in her hands and <u>sat</u> on a chair.

Now look at the revised paragraph. Notice how vivid verbs help convey emotion in the writing and help the reader visualize the scene:

REVISED PARAGRAPH:

Tears <u>gushed</u> from her eyes. Her face <u>flushed</u> red. She <u>gasped</u> loudly, and she <u>snorted</u> as if she couldn't <u>draw</u> enough air. She <u>buried</u> her head in her hands and <u>collapsed</u> on a chair.

HELP with this paragraph:

ORIGINAL PARAGRAPH:

George <u>ran</u> down the street and <u>called</u> to his friend. "I've got it!" he <u>said</u>. He <u>held</u> the five dollars in his hand. He <u>showed</u> the money to his friend. George <u>smiled</u>. He <u>jumped</u> up and down for joy.

REVISED PARAGRAPH:

APPLY this skill in your writing notebook. Replace the ordinary verbs in these sentences with more vivid ones. All verbs are underlined.

1. Sam <u>closed</u> the door angrily.
2. Sarah <u>told</u> him that he'd better <u>move</u>.
3. I <u>knocked</u> on the door, and <u>went</u> into the room.
4. The teacher hurriedly <u>wrote</u> me a note, and I <u>left</u> the classroom.
5. I <u>looked</u> into the binoculars and <u>laughed</u> at what I saw.

MASTER this skill in your workstation.

Word Choice

VIVID VERBS

Verbs are action words, and choosing the right ones can make your writing soar! Every sentence contains at least one verb, so make sure that yours make an impact on your readers by choosing vivid verbs that help describe the mood and feeling in your writing.

ORIGINAL PARAGRAPH:

Tears <u>ran</u> from her eyes. Her face <u>turned</u> red. She <u>breathed</u> loudly, and she <u>inhaled</u> as if she couldn't <u>get</u> enough air. She <u>put</u> her head in her hands and <u>sat</u> on a chair.

Now look at the revised paragraph. Notice how vivid verbs help convey emotion in the writing and help the reader visualize the scene:

REVISED PARAGRAPH:

Tears <u>gushed</u> from her eyes. Her face <u>flushed</u> red. She <u>gasped</u> loudly, and she <u>snorted</u> as if she couldn't <u>draw</u> enough air. She <u>buried</u> her head in her hands and <u>collapsed</u> on a chair.

TASK A For each verb below, think of at least two more verbs that could be substituted to help make a sentence more vivid.

run	talk	breathe	walk	look
write	eat	smell	help	cry
laugh	yell	say	destroy	touch

TASK B Observe what's going on around you right now. Write ten sentences that describe the actions that are taking place this very moment. Underline each verb and, if needed, change your verbs to more vivid ones.

TASK C Write a paragraph describing an emotional event in your life. It can be a happy moment, or it can be sad, exciting, scary, or funny. As you write, make sure that you use vivid verbs that help the reader share in the emotions of your narrative.

TASK D Select a piece from your draft folder or your notebook that could be improved by selecting more vivid verbs. Remember, the purpose of using vivid verbs is to help create a mood in your piece.

Word Choice

Mini-lesson

ADDING ADVERBS

The most common use of adverbs is to modify verbs. Many, but not all, adverbs can be identified by the suffix *-ly*. We're going to look at adverbs of manner, that is, adverbs that show **how** the action takes place. Using adverbs properly adds spice to your verbs. But be careful—like spice, you don't want to overdo adverbs. Use them sparingly, and your writing will take on extra flavor!

WATCH how it's done. Here's the paragraph from our lesson on vivid verbs:

Tears gushed from her eyes. Her face flushed red. She gasped <u>loudly</u>, and she snorted as if she couldn't draw enough air. She buried her head in her hands and collapsed on a chair.

The adverb *loudly* is the only adverb in this paragraph, even though the paragraph contains seven verbs! One more adverb might help. We might have written *Tears gushed <u>uncontrollably</u> from her eyes*, for example. But you want to pick and choose where you place your adverbs, and be sure not to overuse them.

HELP with this paragraph. For each of the underlined verbs, find an adverb that would modify it.

George <u>raced</u> down the street and <u>shouted</u> to his friend. "I've got it!" he <u>exclaimed</u>. He <u>gripped</u> the five dollars in his hand. He <u>gave</u> the money to his friend. George <u>grinned</u>. He <u>leaped</u> up and down for joy.

Raced:

Shouted:

Exclaimed:

Gripped:

Gave:

Grinned:

Leaped:

APPLY this skill in your writing notebook. Add an adverb to each underlined verb.

1. I <u>wanted</u> a new dog for my birthday.
2. My mom <u>sang</u> all morning long.
3. Cynthia <u>looked</u> all around the train station for her cousin.
4. The cat <u>stared</u> at her food bowl.
5. The bus <u>screeched</u> to a halt.

MASTER this skill in your workstation.

Workstation

ADDING ADVERBS

The most common use of adverbs is to modify verbs. Many, but not all, adverbs can be identified by the suffix *-ly*. We're going to look at adverbs of manner, that is, adverbs that show **how** the action takes place. Using adverbs properly adds spice to your verbs. But be careful—like spice, you don't want to overdo adverbs. Use them sparingly, and your writing will take on extra flavor!

> Tears gushed from her eyes. Her face flushed red. She gasped <u>loudly</u>, and she snorted as if she couldn't draw enough air. She buried her head in her hands and collapsed on a chair.

TASK A	Think of at least two adverbs that could be used to modify the verbs below.

run	talk	breathe	walk	look
write	eat	smell	help	cry
laugh	yell	say	destroy	touch

TASK B	Use the verbs in the table from Task A to write ten sentences. Add an adverb to each sentence.

TASK C	Write a paragraph describing a trip you've taken. It can be a trip to a foreign country or a trip to your local market. Your paragraph should contain at least five vivid verbs to help describe the trip. Add two adverbs to your paragraph to help describe the things that you did on your trip.

TASK D	Select a piece from your draft folder or your notebook that could be improved by adding adverbs.

Word Choice

Mini-lesson

USING SPECIFIC NOUNS

One thing that makes writing come alive is the use of specific nouns (nouns name a person, place, or thing). Readers want to know the specifics of the details of your narrative. It's your job to name names!

WATCH how it's done.

ORIGINAL SENTENCE:

The <u>boy</u> ran to the <u>store</u>.

REVISED SENTENCE:

<u>Melvin</u> ran to the <u>comic book store</u>.

In this example, *boy* becomes *Melvin* (common to proper noun), and *store* becomes *comic book store* (adding adjectives).

HELP with this sentence:

ORIGINAL SENTENCE:

The girl wanted a present.

REVISED SENTENCE:

APPLY this skill in your writing notebook. Liven up the ordinary sentences below by using specific nouns. Change the common noun to a proper noun, or add adjectives that describe the noun. All nouns are underlined.

---

1. Our <u>teacher</u> gave us <u>homework</u>.
2. The <u>car</u> raced down the <u>street</u>.
3. My <u>aunt</u> gave me <u>candy</u>.
4. My <u>friend</u> fed an <u>animal</u> at the <u>zoo</u>.
5. The <u>woman</u> ate <u>lunch</u> at the <u>restaurant</u>.

MASTER this skill in your workstation.

Word Choice

USING SPECIFIC NOUNS

One thing that makes writing come alive is the use of specific nouns (nouns name a person, place, or thing). Readers want to know the specifics of the details of your narrative. It's your job to name names!

ORIGINAL SENTENCE:

The <u>boy</u> ran to the <u>store</u>.

REVISED SENTENCE:

<u>Melvin</u> ran to the <u>comic book store</u>.

In this example, *boy* becomes *Melvin* (common to proper noun), and *store* becomes *comic book store* (adding adjectives).

TASK A	From the list of common nouns below, change the common noun to a proper noun, or add adjectives to the noun to make it more specific.

house	TV show	park	city	school
man	dog	clothing	food	book
ball	color	flower	money	woman

TASK B	Make a list of common nouns from the people and things you see around you right now. Then, name names! Change the common nouns to proper nouns, or add adjectives to the nouns to make them more specific.

TASK C	Write a paragraph or two describing a place you are familiar with. Underline all your nouns. Then, change all your ordinary nouns into more specific ones.

TASK D	Select a piece from your draft folder or your writing notebook that could be improved by using more specific nouns. Revise your piece by using more specific nouns.

Descriptive Writing

SENSORY DETAILS

The word *sensory* means "relating to the senses"—in other words, having to do with sight, touch, smell, sound, and taste. Adding sensory details to your writing allows the reader to experience the same sensations as your characters.

WATCH   how it's done.

ORIGINAL PARAGRAPH:

I woke up in the morning. The sun was shining, and my mom was making breakfast. She made me toast with jelly.

REVISED PARAGRAPH:

The sun glared in my eyes through the half-open blinds. I heard the sound of plates and glasses clanking, so I knew my mom was busy making breakfast. I pulled the itchy wool blanket over my head, but the warm smell of toast lured me out of the bed. As I entered the kitchen, I saw my mom slathering jelly on the steaming bread. I took a bite, and the sticky sweetness of the jelly made my mouth water.

HELP   with this sentence:

ORIGINAL PARAGRAPH:

I entered the school cafeteria and looked for my friends. There was a crowd. I got my lunch and squeezed in next to my friends.

REVISED PARAGRAPH:

I saw a swarm of people as I entered the school cafeteria.

APPLY   this skill in your writing notebook. Choose a place you know well, and describe it using sensory details. If you can, try to use all five senses in your description.

MASTER   this skill in your workstation.

Descriptive Writing

SENSORY DETAILS

The word *sensory* means "relating to the senses"—in other words, having to do with sight, touch, smell, sound, and taste. Adding sensory details to your writing allows the reader to experience the same sensations as your characters.

ORIGINAL PARAGRAPH:

I woke up in the morning. The sun was shining, and my mom was making breakfast. She made me toast with jelly.

REVISED PARAGRAPH:

The sun glared in my eyes through the half-open blinds. I heard the sound of plates and glasses clanking, so I knew my mom was busy making breakfast. I pulled the itchy wool blanket over my head, but the warm smell of toast lured me out of the bed. As I entered the kitchen, I saw my mom slathering jelly on the steaming bread. I took a bite, and the sticky sweetness of the jelly made my mouth water.

TASK A Copy the chart below into your notebook. For each place, list things you might see, hear, touch, smell, or taste in that place.

School   Farm   Bakery   Hospital   Supermarket

TASK B For each place listed in Task A, write a sentence that contains at least one sensory detail describing that place.

TASK C In your notebook, write a description of a place (or even a person, if you want to get imaginative!) using sensory details. If possible, use a detail for each of the five senses in your description.

TASK D Select a piece from your draft folder or your notebook that could be improved through the use of sensory details. Choose a specific place or person to describe through sensory images or, if you wish, add sensory details throughout your narrative.

TABLEAU

A tableau is a writing technique that is used to describe a moment frozen in time. This technique is frequently used in theater as a pause between scenes. All the actors freeze in place, allowing the audience to absorb the moment, and then the action resumes.

Writers also use this technique by taking a break in the action to thoroughly describe an important moment in their narrative. Using tableau in your narratives will help bring them to life for your readers by helping them visualize the characters and setting. To create an effective tableau, you must first visualize a scene from your narrative in your own mind. Imagine that you can visit that frozen moment. What would you see, hear, smell, touch, or even taste? What details will help bring that moment to life in the mind of your reader?

WATCH how it's done.

> The door creaked open. A flood of light poured through the doorway. As I looked inside, I could see a strange-looking figure standing at the far end of the room. He was tall but thin, with a jagged red scar running down his left cheek. His piercing blue eyes looked into mine, and I heard him chuckle softly to himself. As my eyes adjusted to the light, I noticed that his fists were clenched and his legs were taut as springs, ready to pounce.

Notice how the writer of this passage described a single moment in vivid detail, using a number of sensory images to bring the tableau to life.

HELP write a tableau with me using this starter sentence:

> The music at the carnival shrieked in my ears.

APPLY this skill in your writing notebook. Look around the room, and freeze the moment in your mind. What images, sounds, smells, and textures stand out? Write a tableau describing the moment.

MASTER this skill in your workstation.

Descriptive Writing

TABLEAU

A tableau is a writing technique that is used to describe a moment frozen in time. This technique is frequently used in theater as a pause between scenes. All the actors freeze in place, allowing the audience to absorb the moment, and then the action resumes.

Writers also use this technique by taking a break in the action to thoroughly describe an important moment in their narrative. Using tableau in your narratives will help bring them to life for your readers by helping them visualize the characters and setting. To create an effective tableau, you must first visualize a scene from your narrative in your own mind. Imagine that you can visit that frozen moment. What would you see, hear, smell, touch, or even taste? What details will help bring that moment to life in the mind of your reader?

TASK A   Create a list of words like the ones below that describe the tableau in your mind. Your list should include nouns and adjectives that describe the people and places you've imagined.

ADJECTIVES	NOUNS
fragrant	flowers
blinding	light
teary blue	eyes
quivering	lips

TASK B   Create a list of words like the ones below that describe the tableau in your mind. Your list should include nouns and adjectives that describe the people and places you've imagined and vivid verbs that capture the action that was taking place at the moment your tableau was frozen in time.

ADJECTIVES	NOUNS	VERBS
fragrant	flowers	dance
blinding	light	flash
teary blue	eyes	water
quivering	lips	pout

TASK C   Choose a place that is familiar to you, and create a tableau of that place in your writing notebook by freezing a moment in your mind and describing it thoroughly with sensory details and vivid verbs.

TASK D   Choose a notebook entry or a piece from your writing folder that could use some description. Find a place where you could effectively place a tableau. After you finish drafting in your writing notebook, you may wish to rewrite this part on a sticky note and place it where it is to be inserted in your text for later rewriting.

Descriptive Writing

Mini-lesson

SIMILES

A simile is a figure of speech that compares two different things using the words *like* or *as*. Similes highlight the quality of the thing you want to describe by comparing it with something that has a similar quality. They allow your reader to "see" what you're describing, and they just plain sound good in your writing!

Tip: Although similes are wonderful tools for description, they should be used sparingly. Use them only when you really want to help your reader visualize something.

WATCH how it's done.

ORIGINAL DESCRIPTION:

The boy was very fast.

DESCRIPTION USING A SIMILE:

The boy was as fast as lightning.

Notice that the two things being compared—a boy and lightning—are two very different things. Saying *The boy is as fast as my brother* is a comparison, but not a simile, because the things being compared are the same—both are boys.

HELP with this sentence. Turn it into a simile.

ORIGINAL DESCRIPTION:

The girl's face was red.

DESCRIPTION USING A SIMILE:

The girl's face was as red as

APPLY this skill in your writing notebook. Take each ordinary description and turn it into a simile by making a comparison using *like* or *as*.

---

1. Jacob was strong.
2. Alison was smart.
3. The day was long.
4. The painting was beautiful.
5. The ocean was blue.

MASTER this skill in your workstation.

Descriptive Writing

SIMILES

A simile is a figure of speech that compares two different things using the words *like* or *as*. Similes highlight the quality of the thing you want to describe by comparing it with something that has a similar quality. They allow your reader to "see" what you're describing, and they just plain sound good in your writing!

Tip: Although similes are wonderful tools for description, they should be used sparingly. Use them only when you really want to help your reader visualize something.

ORIGINAL DESCRIPTION:

The boy was very fast.

DESCRIPTION USING A SIMILE:

The boy was as fast as lightning.

Notice that the two things being compared—a boy and lightning—are two very different things. Saying *The boy is as fast as my brother* is a comparison, but not a simile, because the things being compared are the same—both are boys.

TASK A For all the adjectives below, think of a noun that really possesses that quality. For example, for the word *red*, you might write *rose* because a rose is truly red.

ADJECTIVE	NOUN	ADJECTIVE	NOUN	ADJECTIVE	NOUN
red	rose	small		big	
fast		slow		old	
young		fresh		wet	
dry		fragrant		messy	
sweet		bright		tricky	

TASK B Choose any ten of the adjectives in Task A, and write a simile for each one.

TASK C Choose a person or a place to describe, and use **only** similes to describe it. (Note: This is an exercise—you don't want to overdo similes in your actual writing!)

TASK D Select a piece from your draft folder or your notebook that could be improved by adding similes. Remember that part of the art of similes is using them sparingly where they'll be the most effective!

Descriptive Writing

Mini-lesson

METAPHORS

Metaphors are like similes. Both compare two different things. Metaphors, however, compare those things directly without using *like* or *as*. For example, instead of saying *The sun is bright like a diamond* (simile), you would say *The sun is a bright diamond*. In other words, the thing being compared isn't said to be *like* something else—it *is* something else.

Because metaphors can be difficult to think of, many writers find it helpful to create a simile first and then remove the *like* or *as*. See for yourself how it's done.

WATCH   how it's done.

ORIGINAL SIMILE:
The flowers danced like miniature ballerinas in the breeze.

NEW METAPHOR:
The flowers were miniature ballerinas dancing in the breeze.

HELP   with this example. Turn this simile into a metaphor:

ORIGINAL SIMILE:
The runner was like a rocket as he raced toward the finish line.

NEW METAPHOR:

APPLY   this skill in your writing notebook. Create your own metaphors by rewording these similes.

1. I could read his face like an open book.
2. The baby's skin was as soft as velvet.
3. His imagination soared like a shooting star.
4. The river was like a snake twisting around the mountains.
5. Her mind was as sharp as a knife's edge.

MASTER   this skill in your workstation.

Descriptive Writing

Workstation

METAPHORS

Metaphors are like similes. Both compare two different things. Metaphors, however, compare those things directly without using *like* or *as*. For example, instead of saying *The sun is bright like a diamond* (simile), you would say *The sun is a bright diamond*. In other words, the thing being compared isn't said to be *like* something else—it *is* something else.

Because metaphors can be difficult to think of, many writers find it helpful to create a simile first and then remove the *like* or *as*. See for yourself how it's done.

ORIGINAL SIMILE:

The flowers danced like miniature ballerinas in the breeze.

NEW METAPHOR:

The flowers were miniature ballerinas dancing in the breeze.

TASK A   Change each of these similes into a metaphor.

---

1. The man was as brave as a lion.
2. His feet were like huge canoes.
3. The flower's petals were soft as silky cloth.
4. His winter clothes were like an oven, baking him alive.
5. My pillow was as soft as a cloud as I drifted off to sleep.

TASK B
Take each sentence starter, and create a metaphor using the word in parentheses as your guide. For example, in the sentence *She was (quick) on the race track*, you might write *She was a bullet on the race track*.

---

1. Jonathan was (strong) carrying those heavy bricks.
2. The sun was (bright).
3. This bed is (hard).
4. Simone is (smart) in math class.
5. His heavy steps were (noisy).

TASK C
Think of a person or place you can describe vividly. Describe it using **only** metaphors. Try to think of at least five metaphors to use in your description.

TASK D
Select a piece from your draft folder or your notebook that could be improved by using metaphors. Find places in your writing where metaphors will be most effective.

Composing Techniques: Target Skill Lessons and Workstation Tasks

Descriptive Writing

Mini-lesson

ALLITERATION

Rhymes are words that sound alike at the end. Alliteration is when the beginning sounds of words are the same or similar. Like rhymes, alliteration can make your writing sound more poetic. When alliteration is used effectively, readers won't even know it's being used, but they will "hear" the flow of sounds in their minds as they read. Don't overdo it, though; starting too many words with the same sound can make a sentence more difficult to read.

WATCH how it's done.

ORIGINAL SENTENCE:

Sheila is a great lady.

REVISED SENTENCE USING ALLITERATION:

Sheila is a <u>w</u>onderful <u>w</u>oman.

REVISED SENTENCE THAT OVERDOES IT:

Sheila is a <u>w</u>onderful <u>w</u>oman <u>w</u>ho <u>w</u>ears a <u>w</u>ild <u>w</u>ardrobe.

HELP with this sentence. Change or add words to make it alliterative.

ORIGINAL SENTENCE:

She was wearing a nice white shirt.

REVISED SENTENCE USING ALLITERATION:

APPLY this skill in your writing notebook. Change or add words in each of these sentences to make them alliterative. Underline the beginning sounds of the alliterative words:

1. Julia walked along the street.
2. Edward was tall and handsome.
3. I put on my best shoes.
4. The sky was blue and sunny.
5. The car was fast and stylish.

MASTER this skill in your workstation.

Descriptive Writing

Workstation

ALLITERATION

Rhymes are words that sound alike at the end. Alliteration is when the beginning sounds of words are the same or similar. Like rhymes, alliteration can make your writing sound more poetic. When alliteration is used effectively, readers won't even know it's being used, but they will "hear" the flow of sounds in their minds as they read. Don't overdo it, though; starting too many words with the same sound can make a sentence more difficult to read.

ORIGINAL SENTENCE:

Sheila is a great lady.

REVISED SENTENCE USING ALLITERATION:

Sheila is a <u>w</u>onderful <u>w</u>oman.

REVISED SENTENCE THAT OVERDOES IT:

Sheila is a <u>w</u>onderful <u>w</u>oman <u>w</u>ho <u>w</u>ears a <u>w</u>ild <u>w</u>ardrobe.

TASK A	For each of the nouns below, think of an adjective you can use to describe that noun. Make sure each adjective starts with the same sound.

---

automobile	blouse	flower	house	music
game	dinner	picture	story	teacher
character	person	living room	dog	elephant

TASK B	Write ten alliterative sentences. You may use the nouns in Task A if you wish, or just look around you and describe the people and objects you see in an alliterative way.

TASK C	Choose someone or something to describe, and use alliteration in your description. Go overboard with this—use as many alliterative words as you can think of!

TASK D	Select a piece from your draft folder or your notebook that could be improved by the occasional use of alliteration. Look for descriptive passages that would sound better with a little alliteration. **Don't** go overboard—alliteration works best when it is used sparingly.

Descriptive Writing

HYPERBOLE

Hyperbole is a figure of speech that uses extreme exaggeration to get an idea across. Your reader will know that your description isn't literally true, but he or she will be able to better understand what you're describing. Besides, writing hyperbole is fun! Your exaggerations are only limited by your imagination!

WATCH how it's done.

ORIGINAL SENTENCE:

My book bag was heavy.

REVISED SENTENCE USING HYPERBOLE:

My book bag weighed 5,000 pounds!

HELP with this sentence. Think of as many ways to exaggerate it as you can!

ORIGINAL SENTENCE:

The room was very noisy.

REVISED SENTENCE USING HYPERBOLE:

APPLY this skill in your writing notebook. Take each of the five ordinary sentences below and spice them up by adding outrageous exaggerations! The fun in hyperbole is discovering how outrageous you can get!

---

1. There was a lot of food on the table.
2. I needed eight hours of sleep.
3. I'm really hungry.
4. My sister uses a lot of make-up.
5. Luther can jump really high.

MASTER this skill in your workstation.

Workstation

HYPERBOLE

Hyperbole is a figure of speech that uses extreme exaggeration to get an idea across. Your reader will know that your description isn't literally true, but he or she will be able to better understand what you're describing. Besides, writing hyperbole is fun! Your exaggerations are only limited by your imagination!

ORIGINAL SENTENCE:

My book bag was heavy.

REVISED SENTENCE USING HYPERBOLE:

My book bag weighed 5,000 pounds!

TASK A For all the words below, think of something that really exaggerates that quality. For example, for the word *tall*, you might write *redwood tree*.

smart	small	big	noisy	slow
fast	beautiful	light	strong	nervous
quiet	funny	sad	high	wide

TASK B Write ten sentences that use hyperbole to describe someone or something. Really use your imagination to come up with outrageous exaggerations!

TASK C Write a sentence using hyperbole to describe a skill or ability you possess. Then, take it to the next level by describing all the wonderful things you can do because of this exaggerated skill. (Of course, they will all be untrue—your purpose is to stretch the truth, after all!)

TASK D Select a piece from your draft folder or your notebook that could be improved through the use of hyperbole. Find some descriptions that you really want to make vivid for your readers, and use hyperbole!

Descriptive Writing

PERSONIFICATION

Personification is a technique in which an animal or object is given human traits. Every time you see a mouse talking or a sun smiling on TV or in a movie, you're seeing an example of personification. This technique is particularly useful in descriptions because it helps the reader to visualize something non-human through comparison to a human. Personification will make your descriptions jump off the page at the reader! (Yes, that's personification!)

WATCH how it's done.

ORIGINAL DESCRIPTION:
The snow was falling lightly.

REVISED DESCRIPTION USING PERSONIFICATION:
The snowflakes touched my cheeks and danced as they fell lightly to the ground.

HELP with this description. Think of as many ways as you can to personify this sentence:

ORIGINAL DESCRIPTION:
The wind was blowing.

REVISED DESCRIPTION USING PERSONIFICATION:

APPLY this skill in your writing notebook. Change the underlined words below into examples of personification.

1. The flowers <u>were moving</u> in the breeze.
2. The alarm clock <u>rang</u> and woke me up.
3. The old car <u>made noises</u> as it went down the road.
4. The <u>fierce</u> wind was <u>loud</u>.
5. The volcano <u>erupted</u>.

MASTER this skill in your workstation.

Descriptive Writing

PERSONIFICATION

Personification is a technique in which an animal or object is given human traits. Every time you see a mouse talking or a sun smiling on TV or in a movie, you're seeing an example of personification. This technique is particularly useful in descriptions because it helps the reader to visualize something non-human through comparison to a human. Personification will make your descriptions jump off the page at the reader! (Yes, that's personification!)

ORIGINAL DESCRIPTION:

The snow was falling lightly.

REVISED DESCRIPTION USING PERSONIFICATION:

The snowflakes touched my cheeks and danced as they fell lightly to the ground.

TASK A — Think of as many objects or animals as you can that can be described with the words below. For example, if the word is *dance*, choose objects or animals that could be described as dancing, such as flowers, dogs, trees in a storm, etc.

---

whisper	sing	fall	jump	look
frown	smile	talk	run	cry

TASK B — Think of as many ways as you can to personify each animal or object below. For example, if the object is the sun, you might write that the sun *frowned*, *smiled*, *glared*, etc.

---

ocean	dog	tree	bird	flower
door	camera	river	storm	leaf

TASK C — Write a descriptive paragraph about a person, place, or object. When you are finished, look for places in your paragraph where you could use personification to help bring an image to the mind of your reader. Try to include two examples of personification in your description.

TASK D — Select a piece from your draft folder or your notebook that could be improved by adding personification to a description, and revise your piece.

Descriptive Writing

Mini-lesson

IMAGERY

Imagery is a literary technique in which an image is created in the reader's mind. Effective imagery often uses more than one way of producing that picture. You've learned many methods of doing this, such as using sensory images, similes, metaphors, hyperbole, and personification. Putting these methods together to help the reader visualize what you're describing is what imagery is all about.

WATCH how it's done.

ORIGINAL DESCRIPTION:

The puppy was so cute.

REVISED DESCRIPTION USING IMAGERY (the technique being used in each sentence is in parentheses):

The puppy's fur was softer than silk (sensory image). He was like a cute and cuddly ball of wool (simile). My thumb was three times his size (hyperbole). He danced on his hind legs when I offered him a treat (personification). He was a little bundle of sunshine (metaphor).

HELP with this sentence. Revise it to use all the techniques you've learned:

ORIGINAL DESCRIPTION:

My sister looked happy.

REVISED DESCRIPTION USING IMAGERY:

(Sensory image)

(Simile)

(Metaphor)

(Hyperbole)

(Personification)

APPLY this skill in your writing notebook. Apply all five techniques to the following sentence to create an image in your reader's mind: *I visited a lovely beach.* Label the sentences to show the technique you used in each sentence.

MASTER this skill in your workstation.

Descriptive Writing

Workstation

IMAGERY

Imagery is a literary technique in which an image is created in the reader's mind. Effective imagery often uses more than one way of producing that picture. You've learned many methods of doing this, such as using sensory images, similes, metaphors, hyperbole, and personification. Putting these methods together to help the reader visualize what you're describing is what imagery is all about.

ORIGINAL DESCRIPTION:

The puppy was so cute.

REVISED DESCRIPTION USING IMAGERY (the technique being used in each sentence is in parentheses):

The puppy's fur was softer than silk (sensory image). He was like a cute and cuddly ball of wool (simile). My thumb was three times his size (hyperbole). He danced on his hind legs when I offered him a treat (personification). He was a little bundle of sunshine (metaphor).

TASK A   Rewrite each sentence below using the technique shown in parentheses. For example, if the sentence is *His skin was rough* (simile), you might rewrite it as *His skin was as rough as sandpaper.*

---

1. The bread had gotten hard. (simile)
2. The man was nice. (metaphor)
3. The garbage smelled bad. (sensory image)
4. The book bag was heavy. (hyperbole)
5. The car was fast. (personification)

TASK B   Write a descriptive sentence using each of the techniques you've learned. Label each sentence to show whether it is an example of a simile, a metaphor, a sensory image, hyperbole, or personification.

TASK C   Write a descriptive paragraph in your notebook that uses as many of the techniques of imagery as you can. Challenge yourself to use all five!

TASK D   Select a piece from your draft folder or your notebook that could be improved with imagery. Rewrite the piece with imagery that will create mental pictures in the mind of your reader.

TENSE SENSE

Most narratives are told in the past tense for a very simple reason—the events have already taken place! For your narratives to make sense, the tense has to be consistent, which means that all your verbs need to be in the same tense. Verbs can be easy to identify if you remember that they are the only words that can change tense. Usually, you can add *-ed* or *-ing* to them. Some verbs change form when they change tense. For example, *is* becomes *was*, and *have* becomes *had*.

WATCH   how it's done.

ORIGINAL PARAGRAPH WITH MIXED TENSES:

Raul wanted to go to the park, so he gets his bike and rides there. When he arrives, he sees his friends. They are skateboarding. It looked like they are having a great time. He wishes he had his skateboard with him so he can join in the fun.

REVISED PARAGRAPH WITH CONSISTENT PAST TENSE VERBS:

Raul *wanted* to go to the park, so he *got* his bike and *rode* there. When he *arrived*, he *saw* his friends. They *were* skateboarding. It *looked* like they *were* having a great time. He *wished* he *had* his skateboard with him so he *could* join in the fun.

HELP   with this paragraph. Help rewrite it so that all verbs are in the past tense.

ORIGINAL PARAGRAPH WITH MIXED TENSES:

I woke up one morning and want breakfast. My mom is in the kitchen, but she is doing dishes. I want her to cook! So I go downstairs and asked her if she will make me something to eat. She says she is too busy, and that I should ask my dad. So I did, and he cooks me the best meal I ever ate!

REVISED PARAGRAPH WITH CONSISTENT PAST TENSE VERBS:

APPLY   this skill in your writing notebook. Write a paragraph or two about the events of your day so far. Underline all your verbs, and make sure they are in the past tense.

MASTER   this skill in your workstation.

Workstation

TENSE SENSE

Most narratives are told in the past tense for a very simple reason—the events have already taken place! For your narratives to make sense, the tense has to be consistent, which means that all your verbs need to be in the same tense. Verbs can be easy to identify if you remember that they are the only words that can change tense. Usually, you can add *–ed* or *–ing* to them. Some verbs change form when they change tense. For example, *is* becomes *was*, and *have* becomes *had*.

ORIGINAL PARAGRAPH WITH MIXED TENSES:

Raul wanted to go to the park, so he gets his bike and rides there. When he arrives, he sees his friends. They are skateboarding. It looked like they are having a great time. He wishes he had his skateboard with him so he can join in the fun.

REVISED PARAGRAPH WITH CONSISTENT PAST TENSE VERBS:

Raul *wanted* to go to the park, so he *got* his bike and *rode* there. When he *arrived*, he *saw* his friends. They *were* skateboarding. It *looked* like they *were* having a great time. He *wished* he *had* his skateboard with him so he *could* join in the fun.

TASK A	For each of the present tense verbs below, write a sentence that includes that verb. Then, rewrite the sentence in the past tense.

---

is	see	hear	have	talk	have

TASK B	Write a paragraph or two about the events of your day yesterday. Underline all the verbs, and change any present tense verbs to past tense.

TASK C	Write a paragraph or two describing what you are doing right at this moment. Start with a sentence like this: *I am sitting at my desk and writing in my notebook.* Observe what is going on around you and record these events in your notebook. Write all the sentences in the present tense (after all, the events are taking place as you write!). When you are finished, underline all the verbs, and rewrite the paragraphs in the past tense.

TASK D	Select a piece from your draft folder or your notebook that needs to be revised for consistent verb tense. You may wish to place sticky notes next to verbs that need to be changed to the past tense.

Revision

EFFECTIVE ELABORATION

As writers, we know our own stories so well that we sometimes forget that our readers don't know anything unless we tell them! An important part of writing is elaboration—the process of adding to what we've written in order to give the reader a clearer picture of what's happening. You can practice elaboration by looking for *telling* sentences and changing them into *showing* sentences.

WATCH   how it's done.

ORIGINAL TELLING SENTENCE:

My friend is a wonderful person.

REVISION USING ELABORATION TO SHOW, NOT TELL:

My friend always has a smile on her face and is always willing to help people with their problems. In her spare time, she helps younger kids learn how to read and collects food for the homeless. She's wonderful!

HELP   with these sentences:

ORIGINAL TELLING SENTENCE:

It was a lovely day.

REVISION USING ELABORATION TO SHOW, NOT TELL:

ORIGINAL TELLING SENTENCE:

That kid really gets on my nerves.

REVISION USING ELABORATION TO SHOW, NOT TELL:

APPLY   this skill in your writing notebook. Elaborate on each of these sentences:

1. I love the spring.
2. The music sounded great.
3. The garden was pretty.
4. The guard was really scary looking.
5. The building looked really old.

MASTER   this skill in your workstation.

Workstation

EFFECTIVE ELABORATION

As writers, we know our own stories so well that we sometimes forget that our readers don't know anything unless we tell them! An important part of writing is elaboration—the process of adding to what we've written in order to give the reader a clearer picture of what's happening. You can practice elaboration by looking for *telling* sentences and changing them into *showing* sentences.

ORIGINAL TELLING SENTENCE:

My friend is a wonderful person.

REVISION USING ELABORATION TO SHOW, NOT TELL:

My friend always has a smile on her face and is always willing to help people with their problems. In her spare time, she helps younger kids learn how to read and collects food for the homeless. She's wonderful!

TASK A　For each word below, make a word list that you might use to elaborate on that word. For example, if the word is *winter*, you might list *snowman, snow, sled, holidays, cold, ice,* etc.

---

baby　　　house　　　present　　　vacation　　　car

TASK B　Fill in the blank in each sentence below. Then use elaboration to show, not tell. Add at least a few sentences of elaboration to show your reader what you're describing.

1. One thing I really like to do is _____.
2. My favorite time of day is _____.
3. One thing that really annoys me is _____.

TASK C　Write a complete description of at least two paragraphs on the following topic: *My favorite person is* _____. Remember that your reader doesn't know this person, so it's your job to show the reader why that person is your favorite. Use elaboration to show what's so great about your favorite person.

TASK D　Select a piece from your draft folder or your notebook that could be improved through elaboration. Look first for telling sentences, and decide which ones need further elaboration. Then, rewrite them.

Revision

COMBINING SENTENCES

Combining sentences accomplishes two goals of effective writing: creating variety in sentence length and limiting repetition in word choice. The most common way to combine sentences is to use a coordinating conjunction, such as *and*, *or*, *for*, *yet*, and *so*. There are other ways, however, as you'll see while you practice.

WATCH   how it's done.

ORIGINAL SENTENCES:

My sister is my best friend. My sister is a really nice person.

COMBINED SENTENCE:

My sister is my best friend and a really nice person.

Notice that the sentence length has changed and that the repetition of the phrase *My sister* has been eliminated.

HELP   with these examples by combining the sentences:

ORIGINAL SENTENCES:

Albany is an exciting city. Albany is the capital of New York.

COMBINED SENTENCE:

ORIGINAL SENTENCES:

The day looked awful. The sky was dark. It was gloomy.

COMBINED SENTENCE:

APPLY   this skill in your writing notebook. Take the sentences below and combine them into one sentence.

---

1. The builders worked slowly on the house. The builders worked carefully.
2. Our family has many members. We have aunts, uncles, and many cousins.
3. The tower was huge. It reached up into the sky. It was magnificent.
4. I was happy when my package finally arrived. I was excited, too.
5. The breakfast smelled great. It looked great, too.

MASTER   this skill in your workstation.

Workstation

COMBINING SENTENCES

Combining sentences accomplishes two goals of effective writing: creating variety in sentence length and limiting repetition in word choice. The most common way to combine sentences is to use a coordinating conjunction, such as *and*, *or*, *for*, *yet*, and *so*. There are other ways, however, as you'll see while you practice.

ORIGINAL SENTENCES:

My sister is my best friend. My sister is a really nice person.

COMBINED SENTENCE:

My sister is my best friend and a really nice person.

Notice that the sentence length has changed and that the repetition of the phrase *My sister* has been eliminated.

TASK A — Write two sentences for each noun. Then, combine the sentences into one. Use the noun only one time in the final sentence. For example, if the noun is ball, you might write these two sentences: *I had a red ball. The ball could bounce really high.* Then, combine those two sentences into one: *I had a red ball that could bounce really high.*

House	Car	Mountain	Tiger	Man

TASK B — Write ten sentences about a friend of yours. Each one should begin with the words *My friend…*, as in *My friend is tall* and *My friend is kind*. When you're done, turn those ten sentences into a paragraph about your friend. The paragraph should be no more than five sentences, and you should try not to use the word *friend* more than three times.

TASK C — Write a descriptive paragraph on a topic of your choice. In your first draft, make all your sentences short. When you rewrite it, combine some of the sentences so that some are short and others are longer. Remember, you want variety in sentence length!

TASK D — Select a piece from your draft folder or your notebook that could be improved by combining sentences. In particular, look for pieces that have too many short, choppy sentences. Then use sentence combining to give your revision a variety of sentence lengths.

Revision

SENTENCE VARIETY

Having too few ingredients in a stew makes it bland. Variety adds flavor! The same is true of your writing. Using the same word over and over makes your writing bland. So spice it up by using synonyms, pronouns, and even sentence combining!

WATCH how it's done.

ORIGINAL PARAGRAPH:

Everyone likes John. John always has nice things to say about people. John has some exciting hobbies, too. John likes to ski. John loves rock climbing. John even likes to parachute from planes. No wonder people like to be around John.

REVISED PARAGRAPH:

Everyone likes John because he always has nice things to say about people. He has some exciting hobbies, too. He loves to ski, go rock climbing, and even parachute from planes! No wonder people like to be around such a terrific guy!

HELP with this paragraph.

ORIGINAL PARAGRAPH:

My dad has a car. It's a really nice car. This car goes very fast. I like to ride in this car. This car is red with silver wheels. This is a great-looking car.

REVISED PARAGRAPH:

APPLY this skill in your writing notebook. Revise this paragraph on your own:

I love to play sports. Sports are exciting and fun. I love sports where you have to run around a lot. Winning at sports is important but so is just getting involved in sports. I love a lot of different sports.

MASTER this skill in your workstation.

THE MIDDLE SCHOOL WRITING TOOLKIT | CHAPTER 10

Workstation

SENTENCE VARIETY

Having too few ingredients in a stew makes it bland. Variety adds flavor! The same is true of your writing. Using the same word over and over makes your writing bland. So spice it up by using synonyms, pronouns, and even sentence combining!

ORIGINAL PARAGRAPH:

Everyone likes John. John always has nice things to say about people. John has some exciting hobbies, too. John likes to ski. John loves rock climbing. John even likes to parachute from planes. No wonder people like to be around John.

REVISED PARAGRAPH:

Everyone likes John because he always has nice things to say about people. He has some exciting hobbies, too. He loves to ski, go rock climbing, and even parachute from planes! No wonder people like to be around such a terrific guy!

TASK A   Revise this paragraph so that you use the name Andy only one time:

My best friend is named Andy. Andy is a really nice guy. Andy and I get along very well together. I've known Andy since I was in the first grade. I hope I know Andy when I'm one hundred! Knowing someone like Andy really makes life more fun.

TASK B   Write a paragraph of at least five sentences describing a person you know, but only use the person's name one time. Use pronouns when you need to, and combine sentences when necessary.

TASK C   Think of a hobby or interest of yours that can be named in a single word, e.g., *basketball*, *ballet*, *reading*, etc. Describe it completely without using the word at all. Switch papers with a partner, and see if you can guess each other's interest.

TASK D   Select a piece from your draft folder or your notebook that could be improved by reducing repetition of words. Rewrite those sections using synonyms, pronouns, sentence combining, or all three!

Revision

Mini-lesson

EDIT THE EXCESS

When you're excited about a narrative, it's easy to tell **too** much. Writers often review their drafts only to find that they've put in every detail they could think of. While it's good to describe people, places, and events fully, readers don't need to know **everything**. Part of being a good writer is knowing when to stop and, if you go too far, knowing when to go back and edit the excess!

WATCH how it's done. The underlined sentences are excess sentences. Look at the improvement when we edit them out.

ORIGINAL PARAGRAPH:

One day, I was walking down my street and I heard the sound of a fast car zooming down the block. <u>My brother loves fast cars.</u> The driver had a panicked look on his face. <u>I know how he felt. I've panicked, too.</u> I wondered whether the driver was losing control of the car. He hit the brakes hard, and the car screeched to a halt. <u>I hate loud noises like that.</u>

REVISED PARAGRAPH:

One day, I was walking down my street and I heard the sound of a fast car zooming down the block. The driver had a panicked look on his face. I wondered whether the driver was losing control of the car. He hit the brakes hard, and the car screeched to a halt.

HELP with this paragraph by underlining the excess sentences.

ORIGINAL PARAGRAPH:

Sheila loves to play basketball. <u>Basketball is my brother's favorite sport.</u> She loves to play so much that she dribbles a ball wherever she goes. Once, her love of the game almost got her in deep trouble. I know how awful it is to be in trouble. She dribbled all night, and the neighbors complained to the police. I love police uniforms. The cops only gave her a warning and told her never to do it again.

APPLY this skill in your writing notebook. Think of a person you know very well. Quickly write down as much as you can about this person. Write down everything you can think of about this person's appearance, habits, likes and dislikes, and so on. When you are finished, review your writing, and decide which details might be of interest to a reader who has never met this person. Draw a line through those details that would most likely be excess.

MASTER this skill in your workstation.

Workstation

EDIT THE EXCESS

When you're excited about a narrative, it's easy to tell **too** much. Writers often review their drafts only to find that they've put in every detail they could think of. While it's good to describe people, places, and events fully, readers don't need to know **everything**. Part of being a good writer is knowing when to stop and, if you go too far, knowing when to go back and edit the excess!

ORIGINAL PARAGRAPH:

One day, I was walking down my street and I heard the sound of a fast car zooming down the block. <u>My brother loves fast cars.</u> The driver had a panicked look on his face. <u>I know how he felt. I've panicked, too.</u> I wondered whether the driver was losing control of the car. He hit the brakes hard, and the car screeched to a halt. <u>I hate loud noises like that.</u>

REVISED PARAGRAPH:

One day, I was walking down my street and I heard the sound of a fast car zooming down the block. The driver had a panicked look on his face. I wondered whether the driver was losing control of the car. He hit the brakes hard, and the car screeched to a halt.

TASK A   Copy the paragraph below in your notebook. Decide which sentences are excess, and draw a line through them:

I'd like to tell you about the most interesting person I know—my mom. She does all kinds of exciting things. My dad is pretty interesting, too. She skis, runs in marathons, and has even jumped out of an airplane! Flying in an airplane scares me. One time, she jumped from a plane, but her parachute didn't open. She didn't panic. Two hundred people a year die in parachute accidents. My mom just pulled the emergency rip cord, and landed safely—in a tree!

TASK B   Think of someone you know well. Make a list of details about this person that a reader might find interesting. List as many as you can think of. Now, pretend that you are assigned to write an essay about why this person is a good person. Which details on your list would be excess? Draw a line through any excess details.

TASK C   Think of someone you know well. Make a list of details about this person that a reader might find interesting. List as many as you can think of. Use this list to write a paragraph about why this person is interesting to you. When you are finished, reread your piece and draw a line through any excess details.

TASK D   Select a piece from your draft folder or your notebook that could be improved by editing out some excess. Draw a line through any excess details.

Teaching Resources

Teaching Reports

ESSENTIAL MINI-LESSONS AND WORKSTATIONS

These should generally be taught in the order below and reflect the task and rubric in **Chapter 4**:

OPTIONAL MINI-LESSONS AND WORKSTATIONS

These may be taught in any order, as needed:

ADVANCED MINI-LESSONS AND WORKSTATIONS

For your most advanced writers, you may choose any additional mini-lessons from **Chapter 10— Composing Techniques: Target Skill Lessons and Workstation Tasks** and ask students to apply them to their reports.

Teaching Persuasive Essays

ESSENTIAL MINI-LESSONS AND WORKSTATIONS

These should generally be taught in the order below and reflect the task and rubric in **Chapter 5**:

OPTIONAL MINI-LESSONS AND WORKSTATIONS

These may be taught in any order, as needed:

ADVANCED MINI-LESSONS AND WORKSTATIONS

For your most advanced writers, you may choose any additional mini-lessons from **Chapter 10— Composing Techniques: Target Skill Lessons and Workstation Tasks** and ask students to apply them to their persuasive essays.

Teaching How-to (Procedural) Essays

ESSENTIAL MINI-LESSONS AND WORKSTATIONS

These should generally be taught in the order below and reflect the task and rubric in **Chapter 6**:

OPTIONAL MINI-LESSONS AND WORKSTATIONS

These may be taught in any order, as needed:

ADVANCED MINI-LESSONS AND WORKSTATIONS

For your most advanced writers, you may choose any additional mini-lessons from **Chapter 10— Composing Techniques: Target Skill Lessons and Workstation Tasks** and ask students to apply them to their how-to essays.

Teaching Narratives

ADVANCED MINI-LESSONS AND WORKSTATIONS

For your most advanced writers, you may choose any additional mini-lessons from the "Word Choice," "Descriptive Writing," or "Revision" sections in **Chapter 10—Composing Techniques: Target Skill Lessons and Workstation Tasks** and ask students to apply them to their narratives.

Teaching Literary Responses

ESSENTIAL MINI-LESSONS AND WORKSTATIONS

These should generally be taught in the order below and reflect the task and rubric in **Chapter 8:**

OPTIONAL MINI-LESSONS AND WORKSTATIONS

These may be taught in any order, as needed:

ADVANCED MINI-LESSONS AND WORKSTATIONS

For your most advanced writers, you may choose any additional mini-lessons from **Chapter 10— Composing Techniques: Target Skill Lessons and Workstation Tasks** and ask students to apply them to their literary responses. If you are having students respond to an author or genre by writing in the style of that author or genre, you may wish to use the lessons for narratives as a guide.

The Workstation Progress Checklist

One tool I've found invaluable for writer's workshop is the workstation progress checklist. It lists all the mini-lessons and workstation tasks contained in this book (as well as some blank spaces for your own mini-lessons), along with a place for students to check off which tasks they have completed. This checklist follows the order of the lessons as found in this book, beginning with a section for organizational techniques and followed by a section for composing techniques. The six-page reproducible handout is on the following pages.

Students should be given a copy of this checklist at the beginning of the year to staple into their writing notebooks. As they complete each workstation task, students should note in the corresponding box the date and page in their writer's notebooks where they have completed the task. Using this checklist gives both teachers and students a means of gauging progress. In addition, it can be used to determine appropriate grouping, as students who need to work on the same task can be easily grouped together.

Workstation Progress Checklist: Organizational Techniques

Use this checklist to track the workstation tasks you have completed. For each finished task, write the date you completed the task and the page(s) in your notebook where the work can be found. Attach this chart to the back of your notebook.

Workstation Tasks	Task A	Task B	Task C	Task D
FINDING TOPICS Reports				
FINDING TOPICS Persuasive Essays				
FINDING TOPICS How-to (Procedural) Essays				
FINDING TOPICS Narratives				
FINDING TOPICS Literary Responses				
FINDING TOPICS Narrowing Topics				
BEGINNING TECHNIQUES Dialogue				
BEGINNING TECHNIQUES Setting				
BEGINNING TECHNIQUES *In Medias Res*				
BEGINNING TECHNIQUES Lead Types: Interesting Facts, Quotations, and Anecdotes				
BEGINNING TECHNIQUES Lead Types: Questions, Descriptions, and Bold Statements				

Workstation Progress Checklist: Organizational Techniques

Use this checklist to track the workstation tasks you have completed. For each finished task, write the date you completed the task and the page(s) in your notebook where the work can be found. Attach this chart to the back of your notebook.

Workstation Tasks	*Task A*	*Task B*	*Task C*	*Task D*
CREATING PARAGRAPHS Topic Sentences				
CREATING PARAGRAPHS Supporting Details				
CREATING PARAGRAPHS Time Transitions				
ENDING TECHNIQUES Circular Closing—A Place				
ENDING TECHNIQUES Circular Closing—A Phrase				
ENDING TECHNIQUES Circular Closing—An Idea				
ENDING TECHNIQUES Lessons Learned				
ENDING TECHNIQUES Ending Types: Restate the Main Idea, Make a Recommendation, and Make a Prediction				
ENDING TECHNIQUES Answer a Question, Use a Quotation, and Create a Scenario				

Workstation Progress Checklist: Composing Techniques

Use this checklist to track the workstation tasks you have completed. For each finished task, write the date you completed the task and the page(s) in your notebook where the work can be found. Attach this chart to the back of your notebook.

Workstation Tasks	Task A	Task B	Task C	Task D
CREATING CHARACTERS Showing through Description				
CREATING CHARACTERS Showing through Action				
CREATING CHARACTERS Showing through Dialogue				
CREATING CHARACTERS Realistic Characters				
POINT OF VIEW First-person Point of View				
POINT OF VIEW Limited-omniscient Point of View				
POINT OF VIEW Omniscient Point of View				
WRITING DIALOGUE Credible Conversations				
WRITING DIALOGUE "Said" Stoppers				
WRITING THE BODY The Five Ws of Narratives				
WRITING THE BODY The Five Ws of Non-fiction				

Workstation Progress Checklist: Composing Techniques

Use this checklist to track the workstation tasks you have completed. For each finished task, write the date you completed the task and the page(s) in your notebook where the work can be found. Attach this chart to the back of your notebook.

Workstation Tasks	Task A	Task B	Task C	Task D
WRITING THE BODY CPR—Character, Problem, Resolution				
WRITING THE BODY Conflict				
WRITING THE BODY Narrative Significance				
WRITING THE BODY Flashbacks				
WRITING THE BODY Suspense				
WRITING THE BODY Setting the Mood				
WRITING THE BODY Compare/contrast				
WORD CHOICE Choosing Strong Words				
WORD CHOICE Adding Adverbs				
WORD CHOICE Using Specific Nouns				
WORD CHOICE Vivid Verbs				

Workstation Progress Checklist: Composing Techniques

Use this checklist to track the workstation tasks you have completed. For each finished task, write the date you completed the task and the page(s) in your notebook where the work can be found. Attach this chart to the back of your notebook.

Workstation Tasks	Task A	Task B	Task C	Task D
DESCRIPTIVE WRITING Sensory Details				
DESCRIPTIVE WRITING Tableau				
DESCRIPTIVE WRITING Similes				
DESCRIPTIVE WRITING Metaphors				
DESCRIPTIVE WRITING Alliteration				
DESCRIPTIVE WRITING Hyperbole				
DESCRIPTIVE WRITING Personification				
DESCRIPTIVE WRITING Imagery				
REVISION Tense Sense				
REVISION Effective Elaboration				
REVISION Combining Sentences				

Workstation Progress Checklist: Composing Techniques

Use this checklist to track the workstation tasks you have completed. For each finished task, write the date you completed the task and the page(s) in your notebook where the work can be found. Attach this chart to the back of your notebook.

Workstation Tasks	Task A	Task B	Task C	Task D
REVISION Sentence Variety				
REVISION Edit the Excess				

Class Evaluation Sheet

A class evaluation sheet is a great tool for assessing student needs and for placing writers in appropriate workstations. The sheet should list the name of each student and the skills for which the students are accountable in the rubric. After grading a class set, simply fill in the blanks with the grade of each student for each skill. This takes little time and actually cuts planning time by facilitating future grouping and instruction. Below is an example. A blank class evaluation sheet appears on page 175.

STUDENT NAME	1. Creating Conflict GRADE	2. Realistic Characters GRADE	3. CPR / 4. Five Ws of Narratives GRADE	Mini-lesson Taught: GRADE
John	3	1	3	3
Cynthia	4	1	2	2
Melvin	2	2	3	3
Maria	3	4	4	4
Herman	4	2	4	4
Jody	4	1	3	2
Lisa	2	2	4	4
Katey	4	3	4	3
Megan	3	1	4	3
Robert	3	1	4	2
Louise	3	2	2	3
Peter	3	1	4	4
Luis	4	1	3	3
Armand	1	2	3	3
Lucy	2	1	1	1

Outstanding = 4, Good = 3, Needs Improvement = 2, Not Done = 1

A chart like this gives a straightforward overview of class performance and the needs of your students. For example, it is clear that most students in this class performed well in the area of creating conflicts in their writing. Eleven of fifteen children scored Outstanding or Good in this area. As such, there is no need to re-teach this particular skill as a whole-class lesson. The four students who scored ones and twos can then be grouped together for small-group instruction and further practice in workstations to help build the skills they need prior to revision of their writing.

On the other hand, it seems clear that most of the class needs reinforcement in the area of realistic characters, as only two students demonstrated proficiency in this skill. In this instance, it would be beneficial to return to the lesson through whole-group instruction.

Class Evaluation Sheet

ASSIGNMENT:

Mini-lesson Taught:

STUDENT NAME	GRADE	GRADE	GRADE	GRADE

Bibliography

Freeman, Marcia S. *Building a Writing Community: A Practical Guide*. Gainesville, FL: Maupin House, 1995.

———. *Listen to This: Developing an Ear for Expository*. Gainesville, FL: Maupin House, 1997.

Langer, Judith A. *Guidelines for Teaching Middle School and High School Students to Read and Write Well: Six Features of Effective Instruction*. Albany, NY: National Research Center on English Learning and Achievement (May 2000): 9.

Tomlinson, C. A., "Differentiation of Instruction in the Elementary Grades." ERIC Digest (August 2000): EDO-PS-00-7.

Wilhelm, J. D., Baker, T. N., & Dube, J. *Strategic Reading: Guiding Students to Lifelong Literacy*, 6–12. Portsmouth, NH: Heinemann, 2001.

Notes

Notes